PRAISE FOR *GOD IS NOT HERE*

"*God Is Not Here* sharply details the thorny tensions of our new wars, and how American forces have been thrust into vexing, unwinnable situations. Edmonds reveals how these experiences exacted a ruinous toll on him. It is a story of moral injury—and betrayal—and shows that our service members deserve clear and serious leadership. Without it, they'll have to fight another wrenching battle when they return home."

—Joshua E. S. Phillips, author of *None of Us Were Like This Before: American Soldiers and Torture*

"While our country is deep in conversation about how to help veterans who return from combat with PTSD, a much less discussed topic is soldiers who return with moral injuries. *God Is Not Here* is a courageous memoir that provides extraordinary insight into the challenges of adjusting to normal life after dealing with the moral complexity of combat. A valuable resource for understanding one of the many negative repercussions of torture—the effect it has on the welfare of our own soldiers."

—Tony Camerino, former senior military interrogator, author of *How to Break a Terrorist*, (written as Matthew Alexander)

"America's modern wars have played out in the background for most of America's people. For those who were engaged, the consequences will last a lifetime and are only beginning to be fully reckoned. *God Is Not Here* is a remarkable and eloquent addition to the literature of today's wars, an unsparing assessment of what 'urban warfare' and 'enhanced interrogation' mean for those carrying them out. The country in whose name Bill Russell Edmonds has fought needs to read his account."

—James Fallows, National Correspondent, *The Atlantic*, author of *The Tragedy of the American Military*

"A wrenchingly honest account of a soldier's inner conflicts in a morally ambiguous war. Working with an Iraqi officer interrogating Iraqi terror suspects, Bill Edmonds got what most U.S. soldiers did not: a view of the Iraq war through Iraqi and not American eyes. That perspective gives a painful but illuminating and necessary lesson on the true nature of America's conflicts in our era."

—Arnold R. Isaacs, author of *Without Honor: Defeat in Vietnam and Cambodia* and *Vietnam Shadows: The War, Its Ghosts, and Its Legacy.*

"*God Is Not Here* is an honest, gritty and unflinching look at the war in Iraq and its impact on the human spirit. The writing is crisp and the story is gut wrenching. One of the best Iraq books I've ever read."

—Kevin Maurer, co-author of *No Easy Day: The Firsthand Account of the Mission that Killed Osama Bin Laden*

"*God Is Not Here* is a courageous book by a thoughtful warrior whose personal story shows us the terrible moral and human costs of torture, not just to those who are tortured, but to the torturers."

—Scott Cooper, National Security Outreach Director, Human Rights First.

"A raw portrayal of Faulkner's human heart in conflict with itself. Part confession and part treatise, I was engrossed by Edmonds' ongoing conversations with Saedi, his Iraqi counterpart who serves as both his good and bad angel. It is commendable that Edmonds even attempts to reconcile right and wrong in his impossible role, but it is also the source of the tragedy."

—Brian Castner, author of *The Long Walk:
A Story of War and the Life That Follows*

"An important account of how torture is ineffective and can deeply harm those who merely witness it. A must-read for anyone who cares about America's future and the welfare of U.S. service members."

—Lieutenant Colonel Douglas A. Pryer,
author of *The Fight for the High Ground*

"Heraclitus wrote that 'truth likes to hide.' *God Is Not Here* is about bringing truth out of hiding, the agony of living with it, and finding the courage to tell it. Edmonds' wrenching chronicle of his deployment to hell—his infernal 'descent into a moral abyss'—is required reading for the nation that sent him there."

—Robert Emmet Meagher, author of *Killing from the Inside Out:
Moral Injury and Just War*

"A powerful and courageous story of a soldier's fight against a policy that ran counter to his own moral code. As a young captain, Bill Edmonds was idealistic, excited to do his part in the war on terror. But his embed with Iraqi intelligence forces didn't go as planned. The unit's interrogation practices were brutal. But when he raised concerns about the tactics to commanders, he was brushed aside. In one of the best books written about the Iraq and Afghanistan conflicts, Edmonds provides a compelling glimpse into this dark world where the ends justify the means, and his own heartbreaking struggle to maintain his sanity in the face of immoral behavior."

—Mitch Weiss, Pulitzer Prize-winning investigative journalist
and author of *Tiger Force: A True Story of Men and War* and
No Way Out: A Story of Valor in the Mountains of Afghanistan.

"A truly remarkable memoir. With searing candor and profound soul-searching, Edmonds opens our eyes to the horrible moral ambiguities that he faced. He has no pat answers about living in a space between complicity and moral protest of torture, but the protest that does cry out is that he has lived too long with his own moral anguish. As a nation we must stop distancing ourselves from the Americans who fight on our behalf and start holding ourselves accountable to help them heal."

—Nancy Sherman, author of *Afterwar:
Healing the Moral Wounds of our Soldiers*

god is not here

A SOLDIER'S STRUGGLE WITH TORTURE, TRAUMA, AND THE MORAL
INJURIES OF WAR

LIEUTENANT COLONEL BILL RUSSELL EDMONDS
FOREWORD BY THOMAS RICKS
INTRODUCTION BY BILL NASH, M.D.

PEGASUS BOOKS
NEW YORK LONDON

GOD IS NOT HERE

Pegasus Books LLC
80 Broad Street, 5th Floor
New York, NY 10004

First Pegasus Books cloth edition May 2015

Interior design by Maria Fernandez

ISBN: 978-1-60598-774-3

10 9 8 7 6 5 4 3 2 1

Printed in the United States of America
Distributed by W. W. Norton & Company, Inc.

To the altruists who listened, then lent a hand:
Prof. George Lober, Dr. Cynthia King, Dean Wright,
Joan Connell, LTC Douglas A. Pryer, Bill Nash M.D.,
and Thomas Ricks

To the parents who understood, then steadied a hand:
Bill and Lynn Edmonds

To the family who loved, then held a hand:
Cheryl, Natalie and Ava

Foreword

by Thomas Ricks

Pulitzer Prize Winner and Three-Time
New York Times Bestselling Author

You know Bill Edmonds is on to something from the very beginning of the book, which I think is one of the best to come out of the Iraq war. The dark title is compelling. Then, in his first sentences, he writes that "I'm a good person forced to make many horrible choices." Not only is this true, it is also a powerful narrative device, for he is bidding you to follow him on a descent into Hell. Those who take the dare will quickly find out what some of those evil choices were: "I lived according to Iraqi rules, and I interrogated with only one rule—do what was necessary."

Soon we see him sitting in a dank cinderblock basement prison cell in Iraq, wearing a black mask. "There is no better place to learn about God than from killers who use God to justify their killing," he writes. That one sentence contains an entire journey into the heart of darkness. When I first encountered it, I read it several times. It was mid-2005, a particularly bad time in the war, when American leaders, both political and military, were

1

still deeply in denial about how badly the Iraq war was going. Indeed, as Edmonds observes, much of the massive American military effort in Iraq at the time was counterproductive, simply antagonizing Iraqis.

All told, this memoir amounts to a textbook on psychological trauma. All the ingredients identified by Dr. Jonathan Shay in his two groundbreaking books on the syndrome are here. If the Army in some perverse experiment had consciously wanted to try to traumatize one of its officers, it could not have done a more effective job than it did on Edmonds.

Here's the recipe:

Begin the plunge with a debilitating sense of a loss of control over one's life. Edmonds is a U.S. military officer, but in Iraq he did not command a unit. Rather, he was an advisor to an Iraqi intelligence officer, trying to help by asking questions and giving advice. He feels his moral fate is not in his own hands. Indeed, not even his worldly possessions are under his control, because he has given financial power of attorney to his girlfriend, who lives in his apartment but with whom he breaks up midway through his deployment.

Next, place him in a situation for which he is unsupported and untrained. For example, he seems at first to believe that torture works, something that most seasoned interrogators I know reject. On top of that, his commander is a distant figure, seemingly paralyzed. Lack of competent, caring leadership is a powerful driver.

It gets worse. Dr. Shay has found that one of the most important palliatives for moral trauma is good cohesion among troops. Unfortunately, Edmonds shipped overseas with a small ad hoc assemblage of soldiers whom he barely knew. Less than a hundred days into his year-long deployment, he observes that "I am getting frustrated with the Americans I work with, and I just do not want to be around them anymore. . . . [W]e just all start to go our own separate ways." He is isolated and vulnerable.

Next, put before him what only seem to be bad and worse choices—and make him decide. "I balance between my professional obligation as an American soldier to capture or kill the terrorist and my professional obligation to protect the terrorist that we capture," he confesses halfway through his tour of duty. "I'm fucked no matter what."

Finally, keep the patient's brain on boil with daily jolts of adrenaline. "Knowing that death is so close makes me feel intensely, and intensely living is absolutely addictive," he writes in one particularly effective sentence.

Soon, naturally enough, trauma takes root deep inside of him. "I just don't seem to care anymore, and it's scary to think about how un-scared I have become." By this point, he has lost his faith in humanity: "looking at ourselves, I know the bad outweighs the good."

In his wonderful "biography" of PTSD, David Morris writes that "PTSD is a disease of time." I think that observation is accurate here, and it is reflected in small ways throughout Edmonds' memoir on Moral Injury. We see it at first at about this point in the book, when he is succumbing. "Time just ticks and ticks, and every time I check it seems that no time has passed." This is a symptom, I think, of becoming untethered. I think more research should be done on this crucial aspect of PTSD. As Edmonds writes, looking out at the Tigris River flowing past his base, "Time is like a thick fog that hangs over the river. Living here is like taking a never-ending walk in this foggy soup—time seems to slow and the clarity of events blur."

But the toxic treatment is far from over. Keep the pot stirred with a sense that, as Edmonds puts it, "we're losing this war." That can only make all the suffering and sacrifice seem more inexplicable, and thus more toxic.

Finally, add one more lethal ingredient: a sense of betrayal. When Edmonds decides to report an instance of torture of prisoners, he is at first ignored, and then sees the same people who first ignored him conduct an investigation that clears everyone. "Do we only care about right and wrong when it becomes a media story?" he asks. He doesn't answer that question.

By the end of his tour, he is isolated and alone, brimming over with self-loathing. "I hate myself for giving up," he concludes. Home beckons.

But he finds that when he gets back home, he is just as stuck. He cannot "stop this continual slide into a past that won't say good-bye." Here there are two final kicks: Edmonds is macho enough to refuse for years to seek help, trying to tough it out on his own. And then, when he does belatedly cry out in pain, the Army responds with suspicion and irritation.

Three final thoughts.

This is a very well written book. There are some lines that stay with me, even when I don't understand what they mean. "What is unhappiness?" Edmonds asks in one sad passage. His answer: "It's emotion using reason to understand this world." I don't know why, but I find that sentence unnerving, and tragic. Another comment that struck me is that "dying is addictive." There is wisdom, I think, in his similar observation that "war can become a learned trait, just a habit that you instinctually keep performing." (And as I write that, I wonder if our nation, thirteen years into its "war on terror," has acquired the habit.) There is even a bit of humor in his exasperation with the insurgent sniper who fires at his base all the time, but "can't hit the side of a fucking barn."

This is not a story with a Hollywood ending. Instead, it concludes in a human way, with Edmonds finding a way, he hopes, to live with himself in purgatory. I wish him well.

Lastly I want to express my anger and frustration with our military leaders. They effectively set up Edmonds for his fall. All the ingredients discussed above were already well known to experts on the day that Edmonds flew into Iraq. His leaders failed him. They did not take care of one of their own—not in the way they prepared him for his mission, or supported him there, or took care of him when he came home. More than anything else, this book is an indictment of them. The next time I hear a general say he loves his soldiers, I will ask him if he has read Bill Edmonds' book.

—Thomas E. Ricks

Ricks is the author of five books about the U.S. military, including two about the Iraq war—*Fiasco* and *The Gamble*. He writes "The Best Defense" blog for ForeignPolicy.com and is national security advisor at New America, a Washington think tank.

Introduction

by Bill Nash, M.D., CAPT, MC, USN (Ret.)

Former director of Combat and Operational Stress Control programs
for the U.S. Marine Corps; Assistant Clinical Professor of Psychiatry
at the University of California, San Diego

Reading *God Is Not Here* makes me think of the old e-mail signature of a friend and colleague, the now-retired Canadian soldier Lieutenant Colonel Stéphane Grenier. Below his name at the end of every official e-mail, Grenier sent these words: "For those who understand, no explanation is necessary; for those who don't, no explanation is possible." The thing Grenier referred to—the thing that everyone either understood because they had personally lived it, or didn't because they hadn't—was what happens to basically good people when they are made responsible for bringing goodness to impossibly bad situations. In Lieutenant Colonel Grenier's case, the bad situation was the Rwandan Civil War and genocide in 1994, and the failed attempt to bring goodness to it was the United Nations peacekeeping force in which he served.* No one would have to explain *God Is Not Here* to

---

* Grenier, S., Darte, K., Heber, A., & Richardson, D. The Operational Stress Injury Social Support Program: A Peer Support Program in Collaboration Between the Canadian Forces and Veterans Affairs Canada. In C. R. Figley & W. P. Nash (Eds.), *Combat Stress Injury: Theory, Research, and Management*. New York: Routledge; 2007: 261-293.

Stéphane Grenier—or to his former commanding officer, Lieutenant General Roméo Dallaire, who wrote *Shake Hands With the Devil* about his experiences as the force commander of the United Nations Assistance Mission for Rwanda (UNAMIR), which shrank from 2,548 troops to merely 270 on 21 April 1994, two weeks into the months-long slaughter of upwards of a million Rwandans.* Ironically, the quote Grenier added to his e-mail signature is actually a common misquoting of a statement made by the 13th-century theologian, Thomas Aquinas, describing his belief in God as being so strong that it could not be reinforced by argument or reason any more, one imagines, than it could be shaken by the failure of reason in the face of incomprehensible human destructiveness. Aquinas's version goes like this: "To one who has faith, no explanation is necessary; to one without faith, no explanation is possible." I don't think Thomas Aquinas ever wore a uniform.

God Is Not Here is an extraordinary memoir, both because of the story it tells and because of the historical and cultural context in which that story was lived and then re-examined. I am convinced that the military-cultural context of *God Is Not Here* is one of the keys to decoding its meaning and appreciating its significance. In fact, without that key, some of the wisdom in this book must remain inaccessible. Another key is the concept of moral injury, which I will turn to later.

A very short time ago, *God Is Not Here* simply could not have been written. Barely ten or twenty years ago, there was just too little room in our national consciousness—at least that part of it that pays attention to the military and what it does—for an anguished moral self-examination by a soldier at war, or a frank description of that soldier's subsequent battles with himself. Back then, this book might have read like a disaffected war veteran

---

* Dallaire, R. *Shake Hands With the Devil: The Failure of Humanity in Rwanda.* New York: Carroll & Graf; 2003.

talking out of school. Any Vietnam- or World War II-era veteran considering writing such a book would have been advised by anyone and everyone to *just don't*. "Talk to your friends over beers (lots of beers, if necessary) or talk to your pastor, but don't air your dirty laundry in public. Have you no respect for the uniform?" One concern would certainly have been that such a book would reflect as badly on the military as an institution, and on the nation as a whole, as it would on its author. The author's motives would surely have been called into question; too few would believe that such a book could possibly have been written by someone with a pure heart—someone who was genuinely motivated by his civic duty to share his hard-earned wisdom with the rest of us who never spent a year as an American embedded in an Iraqi/Kurdish military detention facility in Mosul around the same time U.S. soldiers were being sent to prison for what they did in Abu Ghraib. The existence of this book today means that things have changed, at least a little. We are now better able to give the author the benefit of the doubt and actually listen to what he has to say.

What insights have prepared us for *God Is Not Here*? What changes in our beliefs about the world and ourselves have opened us up for the possibilities offered by this book—other than the brutal realities for the military of the last decade and a half? I believe the way for *God Is Not Here* was paved by a growing awareness throughout the West that there truly are limits to human endurance; that war, by its nature, pushes people to and beyond their limits; that bullets and bombs aren't the only dangers service members and their families face during wartime; that no one should ever be blamed for the injuries they themselves sustain while faithfully serving their country, whether those injuries are physical, psychological, or spiritual; and that our national interests are better served by empathizing with our service members and veterans, and listening to them, than by reproaching them for not living up to our expectations or, worse, feeling sorry for them for being weak or unlucky, or whatever curse we think led to their undoing.

I won't list the possible sources of these insights outside the military, though there are many. I believe three groups of war veterans have effectively led attitudinal change *inside* the U.S. military: chaplains, unit leaders, and service members recovering from psychological injuries. To me, military chaplains are *all* bona fide heroes, no matter how well or poorly they do what we ask of them. Imagine serving as the emotional and spiritual advisor and sometimes caretaker for eight hundred or a thousand service members, kids mostly, with whom you literally walk through the valley of the shadow of death, day after day. *Now* imagine officiating at memorial services for twenty or thirty of them over the course of a single warzone deployment. Now imagine how shocked you would rightly be if you actually managed to pull it off—to perform all those extraordinary tasks, for such a long period of time, without once letting your personal needs get in the way or once losing track of what was important. Because they offer to share in the suffering of service members and their families, and join in their struggles to make sense of their lives and service, chaplains can be highly prized in the military. But it is their role as advisors to military leaders, up and down chains of command, that has made chaplains engines of cultural evolution, and teachers of empathy and compassion to some of the toughest people on the planet. Along with mental-health professionals, chaplains have co-led the emerging conversation in DoD and the VA about moral injuries or soul wounds, as they are also sometimes called. (By the way, chaplains did not pay me to say all this.)

The second group of war veterans who have led attitudinal change in the military are a growing number of senior leaders of military units and organizations who have set standards for their subordinates to treat everyone afflicted with psychological or traumatic brain injuries with the same respect and gratitude due them had they been wounded in other parts of their beings, not because to do so served some practical purpose, but because it is right and just. Don't get me wrong, there are still leaders in the 21st-century military who don't believe that service members can be literally damaged by the stress of their experiences in uniform: some still believe in their heart of hearts that "psychological injury" is merely an excuse for weakness or cowardice, just as "shell shock" and "combat fatigue" seemed like excuses to many in the 20th century. (How can we blame them when mental-health professionals, as a group, are far from agreed on this important point even today?) I have known one or two military leaders who reminded me of General George Patton, who was notoriously reprimanded for slapping and publicly humiliating two U.S. Army privates being treated for battle fatigue during the Sicily campaign in August 1943. But now the military can boast leaders like General Jay Paxton, Jr., Lieutenant General Pete Osman, Major General Tom Jones, Colonel Willy Buhl, Colonel Pat Malay, Colonel Todd Desgrosseilliers, Sergeant Major Carlton Kent, and Sergeant Major Michael Barrett, among others. These are all Marines; they made my list only because I know them and have seen them in action. Other service branches are also blessed with such men and women in leadership positions.

The final group of war veterans I want to single out are those who have openly acknowledged having been injured by the stress of war themselves. I vividly remember the first time I overheard two young Marines talking about an Iraq War silver star winner who was also receiving treatment for posttraumatic stress, and even proudly wearing his uniform while getting that treatment. What a shock stories like that were for some, but at the same time a shot in the arm for others. If psychological injuries can happen to bona fide war heroes, they can happen to anyone. A few years into the wars in Iraq and Afghanistan, there arose a succession of senior noncommissioned officers in a few communities of the U.S. military who publicly admitted being affected by psychological injuries, even as they continued to effectively lead troops in uniform. Of course, the American military has no monopoly on the kind of moral courage this kind of self-disclosure requires, as Lieutenant General Dallaire and Lieutenant Colonel Grenier can testify; both have been vigorous advocates in Canada for service members and veterans suffering from operational stress injuries, as the wounds both men received in Rwanda are sometimes now called in Canada. These and other men and women have given others the courage to accept their own stress injuries, and most importantly to take responsibility for their own healing—even if that meant talking out of school.

Someday, I hope to hear service members or veterans talking about how *God Is Not Here* gave them the courage to acknowledge and deal with their own war-related stress injuries.

Now, the book.

One of the first questions psychiatrists ask themselves when listening to others' personal histories, however they are communicated, is whether the person telling the story is a credible historian. Credibility as a historian of one's own life depends on the ability to know the difference between truth and fantasy, and on a genuine commitment to weed fantasy out of the story to the extent possible, or at least to mark as fantastic any untruths that are left in. Consistency is another useful benchmark for credibility: i.e., how well the story hangs together, and how reliably it describes a succession of connected experiences from the same, recognizable point of view. Lieutenant Colonel Edmonds earns my trust and belief in his credibility by his forthrightness about the challenges he has overcome in writing a memoir that he, at least, believes to be truthful; by his willingness to reveal his foibles as well as his strengths; by his unselfconscious spontaneity; and by his willingness to admit that not all of what he tells us makes sense even to him. I believe him.

As a psychiatrist, my next task in reading *God Is Not Here* is to challenge the author's contention that the two timelines in his story are as interconnected as he would have us believe. Were his experiences over twelve months in Mosul, between 2005 and 2006, truly the *cause* of the significant distress he experienced while stationed in Germany in September 2011? This is fundamental. In 2011, the author was clearly distressed and had lost some of his normal functioning. These are two cardinal symptoms of an injury of any kind: pain and functional impairment. But how do we know the mental and emotional wounds that plagued him in Germany were inflicted by experiences in Iraq five years earlier—experienced as the "sharp claws" of his past reaching forward in time, as the author describes in his opening paragraph? Causality is hard to infer in psychiatry. Fortunately, *God Is Not Here* gives us important clues. The themes, images, and impulses that tortured his desperately sleep-deprived brain in 2011 all flowed from painful and undigested memories of Mosul in 2005 or 2006, without exception. This is one of the most ancient principles of medicine: where the tenderness is greatest is likely also where the injury is worst. In psychiatric medicine, traumatic stress injuries (or whatever you want to call them) are one of the few mental-health problems that *can* be causally linked with specific injurious events in the past *exactly* because of the content of their characteristic distressing cognitions and emotions. One of the cardinal symptoms of traumatic stress injuries, for example, is the intrusion into the present of memories of the past that, however distorted they may have gradually become over time, always retain verifiable historical facts. This is not proof positive that the author's two timelines are causally related; but this hypothesis is, by far, the most logical of all alternatives.

If we trust that Lieutenant Colonel Edmonds is telling the truth the best he is able, and if we believe that the two threads of his narrative are truly two segments of the same strand, we must ask ourselves the question he begs us to consider: *What the hell happened to him?* His is not a traditional war-trauma story. Where are the carnage, the dead bodies, the killing, the dying, the terror, the horror? These are experiences that have traditionally been associated with posttraumatic stress, whether they occur on a battlefield or at the scene of a civilian assault, accident, or tragedy. The experience of some form of personal life threat is still a required element for the diagnosis of posttraumatic stress disorder (PTSD), according to the current (5th) edition of the Diagnostic and Statistical Manual of Mental Disorders. The author describes no specific incidents in Iraq in which he experienced a terrifying threat to his own life. Yeah, yeah, he was sniped at, and he was in danger the whole time he was in Iraq, but he was never overwhelmed by fear. He would have experienced very different symptoms if he had been, at any point during his deployment. Instead of loathing and guilt, he would likely have described more anxiety and fear, and his gradual aversion to performing his duties while deployed would have been motivated more by concerns for his physical safety than his moral safety. So *God Is Not Here* is not a story about PTSD. Instead, it is a story about moral injury and moral repair.

Moral injury is a relatively new term for a very ancient idea: that people can be damaged in the cores of their personhood by life experiences that violently contradict deeply held, and deeply necessary, beliefs about themselves and the world. I use the term "violently contradict" to distinguish between moral injuries and the consequences of the more gradual and normal reappraisals of the self and the world we all engage in more or less every day. Moral injury is not some form of damage to beliefs as ideas, themselves, nor is it merely a loss of faith or trust in any particular belief or expectation. Rather, it is a loss of harmonious integrity in the mind, heart, and soul of the person who, over the course of their life, had woven into the fabric of their being the very beliefs that have now proven themselves to be absurd.

Certain beliefs serve as essential handholds for our core selves. Three beliefs, in particular, have been found in research to be shattered in people who were seriously injured by one or more overwhelming life events. These three necessary beliefs are: (1) the world is benevolent, (2) the world is meaningful, and (3) the self

14

is worthy.* In simpler terms, in order to reach our highest cultural potential as humans, we *need* to believe that the world is a good place; that we, ourselves, are good; and that our lives make sense somehow, that they are not just random chaos. Imagine, if you can, how drastically different your life would be if you did not wake up every morning secure in all three of these assumptions. Lose your grip on even one of them, and it could be a long fall.

God Is Not Here describes a few of the processes by which counterinsurgency warfare relentlessly attacks, and sometimes utterly defeats, necessary moral beliefs in warfighters. There are many ways to connect the dots in Lieutenant Colonel Edmonds's story, but here's a succession of possible milestones on the author's road to moral injury. First, he is a special operations officer: an elite warrior in the mold of an ancient champion or medieval chivalric knight, to whom the word "hero" must retain some of its original Greek meaning of "protector." The author was an apple that didn't fall far from the tree planted by his Peace Corps parents. He volunteered to go to Iraq because *he wanted to do good*. Next, the job he was assigned was to prevent torture in a Kurdish/Iraqi jail and interrogation center in Mosul. In the immediate wake of Abu Ghraib, he must have felt that this was a sacred moral duty: to protect and maybe help repair the honor and reputation of America with respect to its treatment of prisoners of war. To do his job, he had to be stationed on a foreign military base and embedded in a very foreign religion and culture where his core beliefs would find few confirming mirrors. To do his job *well*, he had to learn and absorb Iraqi and Kurdish cultural norms and beliefs, just as all effective teachers must begin with empathic understandings of the starting points of their students.

Then, the author's trust in his own moral values—and his belief in the rightness of what his nation had sent him to the other side

---

* Janoff-Bulman, R. *Shattered Assumptions (Towards a New Psychology of Trauma)*. New York: Free Press; 1992.

of the world to do—was slowly eroded, day by agonizing day, by moral dilemmas that he was poorly prepared to meet. The first of these moral dilemmas was the likelihood that humanely treated prisoners would seldom, if ever, disclose the kind of information necessary to find other insurgents before they killed again. Another was the likelihood that captured insurgents who were treated humanely during interrogation would not confess to enough wrongdoing to be charged under Iraqi law, and would therefore be released so they could kill more Americans and, worse, rape and murder more of their own countrymen, including countless helpless and innocent women and children. Back here, in the safety of our comfortable Western homes, such craziness is easy to dismiss as something that, however horrible, is not worth losing sleep over because, heck, we didn't make that mess, and it cannot be our responsibility to clean it up. That may be true; it may not be our responsibility, but only because we recruited, trained, equipped, and then deployed one of the bravest of the brave—an Army special forces officer—to clean the mess up for us. We gave him the broom and dustpan, but we didn't give him any tools that would really work. Yet another moral dilemma was the fact, apparently well-known in theater, that U.S. representatives in Iraq and Afghanistan were not all of the same mind about how much pain could be inflicted in order to get information, about where to draw the line between torture that was acceptable and torture that was not. I am no expert on any of this, so I won't speculate too far; but there are reasons to believe that prisoners who were captured and interrogated by the U.S. military might not receive the same treatment they would receive at the hands of the U.S. State Department, especially if they were hurried off to other countries as part of our policy of extraordinary rendition. I am not interested in the politics of all this. I could not care less. What matters to me as a reader of *God Is Not Here* is simply how these upstream moral choices may have contributed to downstream injuries to the moral identity of a good American boy sent into harm's way to win the hearts and minds of Iraqis and Kurds on the strength of American moral superiority.

One of the author's many insights I want to applaud is his realization that a great role is played in traumatic stress injuries by the accumulation of stress from all other, less-than-traumatic sources piled up over a span of time, as is inevitable in a year-long war-zone deployment. Through the actions of stress messenger chemicals in the brain and body, cumulative stress erodes one's ability to adapt to new challenges as they arise, to sort through options logically, and even to inhibit unhelpful or distracting emotions, thoughts, or impulses. Over time, cumulative stress can actually destroy neurons in the brain that are essential both for making sense out of life experiences, and for maintaining authority over one's own actions. The author hit this target in its central, black ten-ring.

This brings me to the second time span in the author's story: September 2011, five years after he returned from twelve months in Iraq. One of the puzzles in *God Is Not Here* is why it was such a slow burn that apparently degraded the author's mental and emotional functioning over such a long period of time. If he was truly injured by the stress of his experiences in Iraq, why wasn't he at his worst the day he got back? Why did it take so long for his distress to get so bad? The answer to this question can be found in the nature of moral injuries as compared with, say, injuries to skin or muscle or bone. Moral injuries are wounds to beliefs and, secondarily, to the identity of the person holding those beliefs, inflicted by events that violently contradict them. Contradictions between expectations and reality are often not immediately apparent to the person whose brain is laboring to reconcile them. Contradictions and betrayals of trust often take time to sink in, to get past all the compartmentalizing and denial and all the other tricks we use to protect ourselves from such internal dissonance. But as the contradictions sink in—as they are being processed in sleep and wakefulness—cumulative stress not only continues, but

17

it actually grows over time, as the moral meal of war is slowly digested. The author was not at war for just twelve months; he has been at war continuously since he first deployed in 2005.

The greatest lesson I, personally, have learned from reading *God Is Not Here* is the potentially unique role journaling can play in moral repair. We each create our own identities over the course of our lifetimes by building on our innate talents and instincts through effort and experience, trial and error. Tragically, our most prized creations—our own identities—can be dismantled by events that take only a millisecond to occur, even though their full impact may not be fully appreciated immediately. If moral repair is the process of reconstructing one's moral identity after a moral injury, doesn't it make perfect sense that moral repair should also require an act of creation? *God Is Not Here* is a record of the author's re-creation of his moral identity, through the effort and trial and error of reliving his days in Iraq, one by one, until he could find the meaning he needed to really put those days where they belonged, in his past.

Let me close with a few words addressed directly to the author.

Bill, thank you for giving me the opportunity to be a witness to your story, to be part of your chorus, in the ancient Greek sense. I feel honored and blessed that you asked me to write this commentary. I want to leave you with a caution, though—maybe more like a request. Please, please, do not let *anyone* lure you into discussing the political or religious implications of your memoir, if any can be found, as if those are all your book is about. Your message is far too important for that. For the sake of the well-being of our warfighters, veterans, and their families, the only kind of truth that should be gleaned from your book is *scientific* truth: the kind of truth that never knowingly ignores portions of reality just to protect pre-existing beliefs. I know you understand what I am saying, and I trust you won't let me down. One last thing: it's impossible to overdose on chick-flicks. *An Officer and a Gentleman* is one of my personal favorites.

PREFACE

Memories from war never fade. If left alone, they come alive to seep and reach through time with searching and grasping claws. Ignored, they consume, just as they now consume me. So how do I make this right? By rethinking every thought, every word, every choice, and then finally accepting that I'm a good person forced to make many horrible choices—that I made the best of an impossible situation. I will walk out the door. I will move forward. That is my choice. But coming to understand this has been a long journey, and writing *God Is Not Here* is just part of the process. One small step in that direction.

It began in May 2005.

After almost two years of war, the U.S. government finally acknowledged that there was an insurgency in Iraq; if we wanted to win, training the Iraq Security Forces should become a strategic priority. The U.S. military hastily formed a new organization called the Iraqi Assistance Group. I was a Special Forces captain and eagerly volunteered to go to war.

As the first group of combat advisers, we were rushed in to be embedded with the Iraqi Security Forces. I was assigned to live in downtown Mosul—a potpourri of religions, ethnicities, and tribes all seeking revenge for some long-past but not forgotten wrong. I arrived in the wake of revelations of abuse in Abu Ghraib prison. I also arrived at the height of the insurgency and our counterproductive kill-all-insurgents strategy. Mosul was a city boiling over.

My job was to advise an Iraqi intelligence officer—to teach and to temper, but not to give orders. Instead, I was to use my years of experience to point in the right direction. But I did much more than provide advice. Wanting to make a difference, I immersed myself in the experiences. From a makeshift basement prison, over countless midnight and predawn hours, my life became a never-ending cycle—collecting intelligence, capturing insurgents, and then interrogating the insurgents that we captured so we could capture more. I lived according to Iraqi rules and interrogated with only one rule. Do what is necessary. Do what works. Get information and a confession. Lives hung in the balance.

Looking back, I suppose we were successful. We were good at finding, capturing, and interrogating insurgents, and I convinced myself that many innocent Iraqis and American soldiers were saved in the process. But success came with a price. The longer I lived inside of an Iraqi prison, the less certain and more conflicted I became about the right and wrong of everything: absolute certainty is certain proof of absolute ignorance.

In May 2006, I left Iraq with no visible wounds. But something had changed inside. It just took me a long time to realize it.

It began, again, in September 2011.

Exactly ten years after joining Special Forces, and five years after leaving Iraq, my choices finally caught up with me. Over the thirty days of September 2011, something happened. I came to the brink of insanity and quite literally lost my mind. Desperate and within an inch of losing my life, I reached out for help, to both the mental-health profession and my military superiors—and they rolled their eyes.

The mental-health profession said that nothing was wrong, that I just couldn't handle my stress. The military thought me a malingering drama queen and security risk. But both did offer some helpful parting advice. "Write about this experience, that might do some good," offered the counselor. And "Find a new job elsewhere, and be quiet about it" suggested my military superiors.

So I did. I found a new job, moved my family across the country, and began to write about everything. Writing became a way to relive, and relive again, every moment of that year-long deployment to Iraq. Writing became a way to exorcise the demons of my past. Over time, a pattern soon came into focus: my problem—my injury—was not the result of any single event but was instead the slow accumulation of experiences and their cumulative effect. And then I wrote it down, both the experience and my contemplation. Writing became my own very personal form of immersion therapy. It was both therapeutic and traumatic, but it gave me space to breathe and to slowly process, assimilate, and then edit these locked-away memories.

Slowly, inch by desperate inch, I began to crawl out from the abyss. I crested the rim and noticed just a sliver of light in the distance. I took a deep breath, and then looked down.

In my hands I held the pages to a story: the experience of moral injury and the never-ending journey of recovery.

⌒

This account is based on the entries of two private journals, "Iraq: 2005–2006" and "Germany: September 2011." In order to protect my characters' privacy and security, most names have been changed, some experiences and characters are composites, and key memories were turned into illustrations. However, for good or bad, right or wrong, and even the condemning and very embarrassing, this account remains true to my experience.

A central character in the story is my Iraqi counterpart, who I refer to as "Saedi," which is Arabic for "Sir." Saedi had recently joined the newly formed Iraqi Army as an Intelligence Officer. Saedi was also a highly skilled interrogator, a skill he'd honed over decades in the Kurdish Resistance and later as a member of the Asayesh, or Kurdish Intelligence Service. Our life experiences and job positions meant that Saedi and I were in constant opposition—our relationship was best described as one of continual tension. We rarely saw eye to eye on what is "right" when fighting "wrong"; but over time, Saedi and I came to understand that despite our differences, we needed each other. There was one thing, though, that I came to understand and admire about him: Saedi hated the men who terrorized the Iraqi people, and he was devoted to punishing the killers and protecting the innocent. I came to understand and admire this about him.

My parents are also important characters in my story, even if their roles remain largely hidden from sight. Bill and Lynn Edmonds joined the Peace Corps in the sixties. Their first assignment was to teach English in a small Venezuelan village, and after two years they came back to America with two daughters whom they later adopted. Then I was born, then my brother, Jon; many years later, they took in two teenage Mexican girls who were having a difficult time in life. My parents are life-long educators, and between the classroom and their home, they've dedicated their lives to helping those who are less fortunate. Though I chose the Special Forces over the Peace Corps, in some ways these professions are very much alike. Both attract people who are willing to leave the comforts of country and home to immerse themselves in another culture to help those who are less fortunate. My parents now live in Fillmore, California. They are retired, but they have never retreated from their purposeful lives. They still spend their days helping others.

There is Amy, my former girlfriend, an intelligent, ambitious, and motivated woman whom I loved but fought with as the stresses of my deployment mounted throughout the year. When sent off to war, maintaining a personal connection with anyone, especially over distance and differing experiences, can be as mentally taxing as combat.

Lastly, and most importantly, there is my family in the present: Cheryl, my wife, and our two daughters, Natalie and Ava. I met Cheryl only two weeks after my return from Iraq in 2006. She had recently changed careers from finance to acupuncture, a healing profession that relies on a deep connection between the spirit of the practitioner and the spirit of the patient. Cheryl is selfless, empathetic, patient, and forgiving—everything I desperately needed then and now. Seven months after my return from Iraq, she agreed to become my wife. It is my family who keeps me breathing, and it is ultimately for them that I struggle daily to get better.

I was prepared for war—or so I thought. *God Is Not Here* is the account of that awakening. It chronicles a desperate seventy minutes: a one hour and ten minute therapy session with a mental-health professional.

By talking about this personal and painful experience, I hope to provide a "way in" for others in Generation One Percent—the tiny portion of Americans who have served and sacrificed over these last fourteen years (and counting) of war. I hope my telling will inspire them to find their own healing voice. But just as importantly, I hope that by reliving my experience, one of the lesser yet countless examples of sacrifice, Americans will realize that their demands come at irreplaceable expense. Going to war should never be an easy, or easily forgotten, choice.

PROLOGUE

Behavioral Health Clinic: Germany 2011

Day 0

I have a name
What is me?
Takes a seat
Fills out an intake sheet
Enters the counselor's office
Door shuts
Eyes close
To wait . . . for an exit opening

⌐

. . . He kneels and then curls up on the cold cement floor.

"I think he's ready to confess," Saedi quietly tells me.

I'm lucky to witness this questioning, to see this killer slowly lose hope, to give up, and to finally give in. These men deserve every second of misery, and this last emotion, the feeling of "hopelessness" that I now see on this killer's face, is so gratifying to witness. This terrorist's despair brings me joy.

Shoeib slowly rises to sit cross-legged. His head is bent over and he cries. His entire body shakes and he doesn't look up. There is a sandbag over his head and I wear my itchy black wool hood. It covers my entire head with holes cut out for my mouth and eyes.

During interrogations I never wear my U.S. military uniform, and I always wear this mask. This disguise lets me hide, to conceal my identity as an American. Americans have been in Iraq for too long and these killers have learned that we will protect them. They know that an American will hold back the heavy hands of their Iraqi brethren. So now, when I enter a cell, I hide in the dark shadows of deep corners. I become just another Iraqi soldier who takes notes from the rear. Saedi, on the other hand, never wears a mask. He despises these terrorists and he wants each and every one of them to see the power of his crinkled eyes and glowing smile.

It is early morning and the sun has yet to rise. The cell is damp and cold: another long night and morning, and I'm tired. So, from the corner of the cell I pass to Saedi a silent twirl of a finger. Let's start this show.

"How many operations have you done?" he asks Shoeib, and then he slowly rises from his seat to move close. Saedi yanks the sandbag off the prisoner's head, then the question is quickly repeated and followed by a swift and well-deserved fist and foot— Shoeib falls forward to rest his head on the floor.

We already know what this man has done. We just need to hear him admit it. We just need him to confess. He must confess, to declare his guilt with a smudgy thumbprint. Without that admission, this man will just return to the streets to kill again. But fortunately not Shoeib—he is now broken and will confess at any moment. I just know it. So all the hitting and kicking now serves only to quicken the inevitable and to regain his wandering attention, to divert his thoughts back from the sanctuary of self-pity where killers retreat when they've been captured, when they lose their power, when they no longer have control over some innocent's life. Today's abuse is not only a tactic to get a confession; there is also personal satisfaction.

I smile and nod to my partner.

"Speak!" Saedi screams. "If you talk, I may not spend all my time focusing on you. . . ."

And Shoeib quietly begins.

"I have done ten operations," he says with lowered eyes and pitiful sobs.

"What type of operations?" demands Saedi.

"Cutting off the heads, or killing them by a bullet to the head."

Saedi and I just sit there and glare—for almost a minute we let the silence become a deafening roar—and then the questions start again.

"Describe to me your operations."

"In four operations, my job was to hold the legs of the person. I was to keep them still and to stop them from kicking. Six times I was told to do the killing myself. I would either cut off his head or shoot him in the back of the head."

"Who were these people you killed?" Saedi asks in soft loathing.

"I don't know. I would get a call from Mohammed. He would tell me to be at a certain house. Mohammed and some other people I don't know would kidnap someone and bring them to the house. They would tell me to hold the legs or do the killing myself as they made a videotape."

"But who were these people you killed?"

"I don't know. I am not told the names of the people."

"So why then did you do this?"

"I was paid fifty dollars."

Schoeib starts to cry and then he raises his hands above his head and wails, "Wa-Allah, Saedi, Wa-Allah!" and from only a few feet away I feel the shimmers of evil come off this man, this same man who dares to sit here and plead for God's help. Well, God is not here.

I have been here, listening, watching, and participating in these interrogations for what seems years, and night after night these men confound me with their details, with their various acts of inhumanity. I try to stop my slide into their darkness, and so far I've succeeded, barely; but tonight is different. Tonight, when Shoeib wails for some higher power's assistance, I feel a fracture slide down the center of my chest. Tonight, for the first time in my life, I passionately, fervently want to kill another human being. I want to reach across this small prison cell and let my shadow fly.

As I feel my darkness intensely and taste this killer's pleas, I can hear everything, even the now-silent prayers of his victims. I can see everything, every drop of moisture that slides down the cinderblock walls. I hear perfectly, every breath, every heartbeat and every shuffle of booted feet. I'm conscious of every scent, and the odors speak of the excitement, the anticipation, the fear, and the hatred that we all feel. Then suddenly it vanishes.

I feel a deep loss.

I despair.

I need to escape.

I must escape or I will become lost.

I quickly leave the cell and climb the stairs to the roof. Outside, the sun is just beginning to rise. Mosul is beautiful in the early morning and I need a few minutes to just stand here, to gaze out over the city. I need only few minutes in the crisp early light. I need the rebirth of a sunrise. But this morning's peace escapes me, so I quickly descend to rejoin Saedi.

As I enter the cell, Saedi is bent over the still-crying prisoner. He whispers in his ear and cigarette smoke escapes his nose to float up in the air to twirl around the one hanging light bulb. I hear more sobs, which become suckling whimpers. Fucking pathetic.

God, I want to hurt, to kill, this man who takes innocent life and then pleads for our mercy. God, I desperately want to give in, to forget about such things as wrong and right. In Iraq, on these streets and in these cells, such clear distinctions have taken flight. Past rules of the civilized seem childish, completely irrelevant to this new life. Now I just wander without any guiding light and so I close my eyes. I give in, and, in give I.

I become a man I no longer recognize. I've lost myself.

⌐

"Why are you here? The intake sheet doesn't mention specifics."

The voice comes out of nowhere. It's out of place and surprises me but hints, suggests that I've swollen and floated to the surface. I open one eye and the blue is painful.

Then I realize I need to find another human in the rising and falling remoteness. Where is a hand? . . . and then I see a man. He enters the exit to step on a carpeted floor, and I look up to see a poster on the wall, several posters, the same posters on *Determination, Inspiration, Teamwork,* and *Confidence* that hang in so many doctors' offices. As my mind adjusts from the prison's dark, the fog begins to clear.

"Why are you here?" the man repeats.

I'm confused, but I then remember.

I'm in a counselor's office.

I'm in Germany.

It's September.

The year is 2011.

I slip out of the present so easily and so often now that I hardly notice and am often shocked by a sound or touch. Like now: from a basement prison cell and a killer who I desperately needed to kill, to then find myself floating in this doctor's office chair. The echoes are so real, and even now I hear the screams and want to slide into dark corners. I look down to the center of my chest, to search for the crack that must be there, somewhere.

And what is he asking?

"Major Edmonds, why are you here?"

"I need help. I'm fucking desperate." But the words are trapped and I can't say them. So instead I whisper "There is Iraq, which was six years ago. Then there is the present, in September 2011. Where do I start?"

"Tell me what you want. Whatever you think important. The order doesn't matter."

There are too many things happening to me, too many things going wrong, and I'm scared. It's been going on for almost one month now. I no longer have an appetite. I've lost over fifteen pounds and I'm not trying. I barely eat anything at all, yet I still feel filled with energy. I'm not sleeping. I get only a few hours of sleep a night. I wake up early, really early, every morning, and can't fall back to sleep. And when I do wake up I don't feel tired. I feel full of energy and excited until suddenly, sometime later in the day, I slump down exhausted, to fall asleep in a chair or on a nice patch of soft green grass. And my stomach really, really hurts. Then there are the headaches, intense head-aches that come on so suddenly and from nowhere; the pain sits right here, right behind my right eye, and it thumps, and thumps, fuck, fuck, fuck . . . and makes it difficult to think.

But these words echo on my inside. What I have the nerve to say is "I can't sleep. I wake up early and feel exhausted all day. And I feel awful. My stomach hurts and I have intense headaches." Then I go quiet.

I rest my hands on my head, knowing that if I'd really told the truth, about everything, about all of my physical symptoms, I would connect the dots to some rare and fascinating ailment that is the cause of my fucked-up thinking; a brain tumor, perhaps? But no, life is never that easy, because there is so much else that is going on, so much that is happening, so much that I am thinking, so much that I am feeling, and so much that I can't talk about but . . . God, I have to. I have to tell someone. I have to: if not for me, then for my family.

"Is that all?" he asks.

No.

"I am constantly thinking about Iraq. About everything," I say, and then go silent. But if you press an ear to my chest, you can hear the details.

There are flashbacks: the constant flood of memories when I'm both asleep and awake, the ever-present permeable membrane between past and present that I wade through day in, day out. The relentless stream of thoughts that ricochet around inside of my head; the thoughts that hop, jump, and leap from topic to topic. Fuck! I'm constantly thinking, and it never stops! I even have insights into math, physics, economics, metaphysics, and religion, topics in which I have never before been interested and in which I have no formal education, and I know my insights are important, amazing, and world-changingly profound. I am growing and evolving; new abilities are emerging. I am getting smarter. I can just feel it. My IQ has gone from average to off the charts. My personality is drastically changing. I've gone from a quiet introvert to someone who wants to socialize, to interact with people in languages I hardly know, to sit down for no other reason than to have a conversation, to look into another person's eyes and appreciate their triumphs and sympathize with their weaknesses. Me? For the first time in years, suddenly I can feel? That isn't me.

Whatever is going on is making me excited, depressed, happy, and scared to death, but you know what? Of all the things that are happening, what terrifies me the most is how telling the truth will affect my job, my profession, and the respect of those at work. If I lose my security clearance, how can I take care of my family? I wouldn't know what to do.

But these words are trapped and my surface stays silent.

He nods. "Okay. You're constantly thinking about Iraq. And you're not feeling well." His legs are crossed and a notebook rests on the arm of his chair.

"Anything more?" he asks me.

Yes. It's obvious he doesn't hear me shouting.

Because lately, I've started to imagine doing something really, really stupid, like jumping off a cliff or driving the car off the side of the road . . . there I am, hands on the wheel, and I see a tight corner approaching. My speed stays constant and my hands stay locked on the 10 and 2. I close my eyes and I imagine myself floating. I am smiling. There is no fear, and I feel a . . . release, a weight lifting, and well, I just feel. It's a satisfying feeling and it reminds me of how I felt in Iraq, how it felt to stand up in the turret, with my head exposed, with death all around. Does he realize that dying is addictive?

But no, of course he can't understand me, so I don't tell him about these ideations. I barely even whisper them to myself.

"What?" I ask as I raise my head, as I'm pulled back from the car that is crashing through a roadside barrier, and floating. . . .

"I asked," says the doc, "if there was anything more you want to talk about."

What an ass. No, I don't "want" to talk anymore.

"Major Edmonds? Is there anything more?"

Yes, there is so much more, but I don't know how to put Iraq into words. I don't have the words to describe that inner fight, how my many selves struggled to navigate a year-long moral minefield. How every day I was forced to make a choice—do I torture another human being, or not—and how every day, over and over again, no matter the decision, I made a soul-crushing wrong choice, and how the other stresses of war, the daily expectation of death, the failing war strategy, the isolation, the austere environment, and the girlfriend back home, how these other things only compromised my mental immunity, lowered my resistance. Over time, my mind slowed, and then I just . . . turned off. I shut down.

When something hurts so badly, it eventually stops hurting, I want to tell this mental-health professional, and then I want to continue: *but five years after Iraq, something unexpected happened. I felt that entire year all 365 days—in an instant, and for the last thirty days, for this entire month of September 2011, I've been in a fight to the life. And I'm losing. I have a family I desperately love. Can you help?*

But no, my inner chaos doesn't show. There's not a ripple. I'm a practiced professional.

"Major Edmonds." The expert interrupts my silent navel-gazing, my whimpering. "I can't help if you don't say anything."

And so I reach for any courage that remains . . . I have to.

For the next hour or more, I try to describe the back-and-forth between Iraq and the present, these two timelines that are tangled and twisted: the 365 days in Iraq and the thirty days in the present. How my many selves are running, merging, then separating, and sprinting, continuing relentlessly, until they meet at one moment in time . . . .

Whisper softly, inside
About the pendulum swinging,
Slowing. The leaves growing.
I am midway lost, alone
And stunned.
My feet don't stir.
It's the panic inside.
It stretches in this fearful place
Where the past is present,
And alive . . .

Prologue: He confessed to beheading kidnapped Iraqis for $50

One early morning, Shoeib retold his killings, and then begged for God's mercy. At that moment, something happened: I felt a crack in the center of my chest. I saw my shadow fly. For the first time in my life, I desperately needed to kill another human being.

Prologue: My Iraqi counterpart
It was hard to see eye-to-eye with Saedi—on what's right when fighting wrong. But I understood and respected him. He was me, with a different life experience.

Iraq 2005

365 Days Remain

I hunger for the field that will test my mettle. I am here now, and excited.

I wipe the sweat from my brow and admire the columns of black smoke in the distance, the sound of near and far gunfire. The change is thrilling, for just one month ago I was sitting in a bistro called La Tomate in downtown D.C., where I broke the news to Amy: I'm going to Iraq.

Amy and I had been going out for just over a year; but for the better part of that year it was a long-distance relationship, held together by countless hours of driving. Eight months ago, she quit her job and moved up from Georgia. We lived together in a tiny, and too-expensive, one-bedroom condo that I had just purchased at the height of the housing bubble. Then soon after that, I volunteered for this deployment and was excited—thrilled, in fact—that I was going to war, but I wasn't going to tell her that I wasn't forced to go to Iraq. She wouldn't understand the motivations that drive a professional soldier. Instead, I just sat there on a barstool, holding her hand, listening to the mindless D.C. chatter.

She began to cry.

I squeezed her hand and told her I understood; but in fact I didn't.

I was embarrassed because she was making a scene, and it seemed false to me, forced, even a bit clichéd. Still, I tried to comfort her, to hold her tight, to remind her that I'm a soldier and that it's important that I do my part in this fight.

And now only one month later, I'm here on the tarmac of the Baghdad International Airport sitting on the crumbling concrete of an Iraqi loading dock—a world apart from that chic bistro.

It's been a slow start and I'm realizing it's boring, just sitting here, waiting. I look around and within every blessed sliver of shade are soldiers, some sitting, some standing, and many just lying down interspersed among hundreds of bags of every shape and shade of green and brown. I have no idea what's in store for me, but I imagine that my boredom will soon be over. Soon I will be living, sharing meals, sleeping, and fighting insurgents beside some Iraqi. I know that in that future, my complaints will be petty and this boredom will be the least of my worries.

But really, I am excited. I've dreamt of this.

In Special Forces School, we were raised on the legends who did exactly this: lived within another culture in order to fight and kill an enemy from within. I need to get up off my ass to put my training into practice, so I go in search of a few Iraqis to practice my Arabic.

I find them around the corner. I make eye contact. I smile. I put a hand to my chest. I repeat the words I've practiced: *Salaam Alaikum*. I repeat a few more basic sayings such as "Hello"; "Where are you from?"; "How is your family?"; and "Stop! Or I'll shoot!" I sense they're not interested, so I walk back to my concrete loading dock, and then I hear the call to prayer from the local mosque. This sound is a painfully annoying clatter.

But I'm not conflicted about this. Four years ago was 9/11 and I am happy, eager in fact, to meet some equally fanatic Islamic terrorists, and to then kill them. And I will. I will also live with Iraqis. I will work with them. I will eat with them. I will fight with them. I'm looking forward to this. This war is the culmination of a lifetime of training.

A truck finally arrives and moves us to a dusty and thankfully air-conditioned tent. I choose a cot, quickly rat fuck my duffel, searching for a towel and soap, strip off my sweat-soaked and dirty clothes, and walk half-naked in flip-flops across a mile of searing gravel to take a warm shower.

Now, clean, dressed, and sweating, I leave the tent to roam the base in 7 P.M. heat—where is that damn computer room so I can write an e-mail? An hour later, I finally find it in a tan tent hidden in a sea of identical unmarked tan tents. I walk in, scan the room, and make fleeting eye contact with dozens of similarly clad, hot, and sulking soldiers and the only sound is the chug of a feeble air conditioner, struggling and losing the battle. I write my name on a list and take a seat. I wait. And wait. And wait.

Finally, my name is called. I now have thirty minutes to write my family, some friends, and Amy, but already twenty minutes are gone—no, stolen—by an ancient computer with a slow Internet connection. But I have ten minutes left and I am finally reading my first e-mail. Does Amy realize that the first e-mail I read is always from her? Does she understand how difficult this simple task is—the task of connecting with loved ones I left behind?

I want to tell her I am sorry for the argument we had over the phone last night. Sometimes it feels like for every word we share, there are two hidden messages I am supposed to uncover. And when these clues are discovered, they lead to predetermined responses that I am expected to utter. But damn it, I can't interpret her; and when I say what she didn't want to hear, it means I just don't care.

But I do care. It is just that over so much distance, there is so much that we both can't hear. What I want is to bond with her, to talk about more than just chores, to give her a sense of my reality. Somehow this keeps me connected with her and, hopefully, her with me.

Tomorrow, I head out of the gate to where the enemy lives to do what the Army calls a Traffic Control Point. This is my first real operation in Iraq. This TCP is similar to the surprise drunk-driver inspection point that the police do back home, but here we're not looking for drunks; here we seek out the insurgent who hides a bomb or a gun. I hope to learn something by going out and watching other soldiers do this, and I hope to do it right, for last night on the phone with Amy all that I could think was "What if I these angry words are our last words?"

Germany, September 2011

30 Days Remain

It's early and still so dark. I try to rise, but the memories take over. I close my eyes and collapse back into my pillow to feel the cold-leaching cinderblock prison walls, the smell of cigarette smoke, the sobs and the pleas and the open-palm slaps against exposed cheeks, and the omnipresent sensation of drowning. The hatred, evil, and guilt are so thick, it's difficult to breathe; even here, years later, these sensations seep and reach through time with their searching and grasping claws.

So I keep my eyes closed and try to turn my brain off: I don't want to remember all of the guilty—and innocent—people I've hurt because I couldn't *see* the right choices in front of me.

Why is this happening? I sense a distant small voice that whispers "you need help"; but at the same time I know deep down that this is something I can only do for myself and that no matter how real Iraq, that basement cell, those guilty and innocent prisoners, my weakness, may feel right now, what I *really* feel and fear is. . . .

"Don't focus on what you can't control. Just breathe," I tell myself in a before-dawn bedroom whisper.

I open my eyes in the dark to watch Cheryl, who is breathing next to me. She reminds me how it's supposed to be. It's simple and uncomplicated. So just breathe.

I swell my chest to take a deep breath, try to rise from bed, to plant my feet, to take a small step . . . and suddenly I spin; the world is completely out of my control.

Iraq, 2005

358 Days Remain

I haven't heard from Amy for several days now. Doesn't she realize how important her words are? E-mails are a reminder of a real life, a different place, of a world that I so eagerly left behind but can't seem to forget.

She spends her day connected to a computer; can't she spare a few minutes for me? Damn it, I spend hours trying to find a computer, waiting my turn, waiting for a connection, and then I write in order to share a portion of my life; the least she could do is pretend to listen. She knew that I had to travel a dangerous route last night, to a new base on the other side of Baghdad. Did she not even wonder if I arrived safely? But if I voice my hurt, she will get defensive, and things will just get worse. So instead, I focus on something else.

Tonight, a soldier from a different unit was killed. He was driving the same route that I had just taken, just at a later time, and my response was relief—even, oddly, pleasure. Should I tell her about this feeling of "relief" I have when a soldier dies? Should I describe how this response disturbs me? I wonder if my thoughts are even about the dead soldier at all? If everything is destiny, why have emotion at all?

Was it that particular soldier's death, or just a death that was unavoidable? Was that night on the streets of Baghdad just some-one's, anyone's, time to be called? I have been here only a long week, but already I feel the tug of mortality. Being close to death opens my eyes to a greater and indifferent universe and puts living into perspective. I am tiny and insignificant—it just is and I just am—which provides relief for some reason.

I realize I haven't been typing, only staring at the computer screen, and that I have a time limit and others are waiting, and watching. I don't think I will share these thoughts with Amy. I'll just work things out for myself.

～

I wake up to the sound of wheels crunching stone. As I part the tent flap, I see the second half of my unit arrive. They took the same route the dead soldier and I took last night, but they took the route a few hours later than us. Their lead vehicle was a big Army truck, and it turns out that the gunner from another mili-tary convoy mistook their lead truck for an enemy vehicle. They shot at it.

As I stare out from the inside of a tent flap, a friend opens the HUMVEE passenger door, unbuckles the seat belt, unbends one, then two legs to stand and unplug his headphone, and grabs his rifle. He yells "it was just after midnight, for fuck's sake! How the hell do you mistake a convoy of military vehicles, the only vehicles on the road, for the enemy?"

As I fell to sleep in the darkness of last night, two military con-voys met on the empty streets of Baghdad, and the other soldiers shot. "It just goes to show you how pumped up on adrenaline most soldiers are," I tell him, but keep my other thoughts to myself: "They are teenagers, and they're scared, so forgive them."

Norwood Library
4550 N. Peck Rd.
El Monte, CA 91732-1998
Phone: (626) 443-3147

Title: God is not here : a
soldier's struggle with tortu
Item ID: 0112435583300
Date charged: 7/24/2017,
14:06
Date due: 8/14/2017,23:59

Total checkouts for session:
1
Total checkouts:1

Renew your Items online.
Log in to: www.
colapublib.org

"Luckily, only a front tire was blown," he grumpily informs me. "The fucking problem was that the truck did not have any gear to fix the flat." So the whole unit, some thirty vehicles long, had to wait for two hours on the streets of Baghdad while gear was found and the tire was changed.

Later, as we play a game of chess, he tells me that dozens of Iraqis came out of their homes to set up lawn chairs, and to watch this deathly dance. They were having a tailgate party, what with the chairs and blankets and drinks and kids playing and men smoking and talking.

My God, I can feel the sheer panic at the helpless inability to just go, to leave the place that soon will become the scene of an attack, because deep down you just know that an attack will soon materialize. The only question is when and from which direction. Will it be a pot-shot from a roof, then two, and then grow into a crescendo? Or will word spread by phone to the waiting driver of a suicide car bomb? But no matter how hard you pray, you know word will eventually spread and the message will be "American soldiers, in vehicles, broken down, just sitting, all alone. Let's go."

I look down at the game of chess we're playing, and I choose to risk my queen; "Check," my competitor claims.

Last night, beyond all reason the tire was changed and my friend's convoy began moving. They were able to return to base, safe and without another incident or an attack materializing, and I imagine a macabre scene of Iraqis in lawn chairs standing up to stretch, groaning, and feeling disappointed for the lack of entertainment.

After more than one week of waiting, training and equipping in Baghdad, I've finally arrived to Mosul. But damn! The drive up from Baghdad took longer than I ever expected.

We were supposed to leave around midnight; but in order to prepare for our departure, our day began much earlier. We dedicated the day to getting our new vehicles and equipment ready for the drive up to Mosul, because a five-minute drive or a seven-hour drive is the same thing. No matter the distance, if we have to leave the safety of razor wire, if you leave the American base, we must prepare for any contingency. So the entire day—yesterday—was spent packing the HUMVEE.

Everything has to be in just the right place, which is not as simple a task as it may seem: 1) The vehicle has only so much room, and you only want to take what is important (gas, water, ammo, your personal bag, tow ropes, etc.); 2) You have to make sure everything is in exactly the right spot (i.e., everyone must know where our first-aid kit is, and all the vehicles must have the first-aid kit in the same location and it must be easily accessible); and 3) You do not want anything loose or non-essential in the cab of the vehicle (anything loose is something that will ricochet throughout the vehicle when we get hit by an IED). So we pack the vehicle from 0800 to 1300, and then we all strip down to our sweat-soaked brown T-shirts and get to work carrying all of the stuff that could not fit in the HUMVEE to load in a large brown truck. The truck will be sent to find us sometime in the future. That was from 1300 to 1500.

Then came lining up the vehicles, all in logical order. This is another one of those seemingly easy tasks that evolves into a mission as complicated as a NASA shuttle launch: forty-two vehicles, a hundred-some people, ninety-five of whom are in charge, and all of whom have an opinion on the importance of each vehicle's correct position in a line. I sit in my HUMVEE and read a book, choosing not to insert leader number ninety-six in this clusterfuck. That was 1500 to 1900. Then there were the patrol briefings, vehicle checks, communication checks, and all the other drills you must rehearse and then hope to never use.

For example: towing your vehicle. Hooking up a rope to pull a broken-down vehicle is a deceptively simple task until you factor in the recently exploded bomb, the requisite chaos, and the people who are trying to shoot you.

The time is now 2330. The vehicles are finally lined up, last-minute checks are complete, and my machine-gunner is up in the turret at Kevlar defilade. This is Army-speak for "only his eyes peek out over the quarter-inch of armor of the turret." The gunner is the real security of the vehicle; but by being our security, he is also the most vulnerable. I am in the VC (vehicle commander's) seat, and I feel like an anchovy. With my personal armor on, adding fifteen inches to my circumference, my rifle resting beside my legs, the three large radios touching my left arm, the two-inch-thick bulletproof glass kissing my right cheek, my Kevlar helmet with night-vision goggles scraping the roof, and my seatbelt strapping me in, that literally, it is so tight that my legs are forced together and my knees are touching. I am truly unable to spread my legs any farther apart. Now imagine that you are the driver and you have all of these impediments, but that you also have the steering wheel three inches from your chest.

As the VC, I am theoretically in charge of the vehicle, but it's the driver who must make split-second decisions during an attack; so really how much control do I have? And if there is an attack? God forbid that you ever ask me to leave the vehicle; it will take me several life ending seconds, and that is assuming I don't stumble head-first onto the ground with my feet entangled in my rifle sling or in the panic forget to unhook my seatbelt. As I sit here waiting, reading a book, I have these images of hysterically trying to figure out why the hell I can't exit the vehicle.

So we are all lined up and we begin driving out the gate with our line of 42 vehicles. Then one of the gunners on the top of the vehicles accidentally shoots his machine gun. Fuck. So the entire line stops as the gate guards try to find out who the dumbass is who accidentally shot his .50-cal machine gun.

And as we stop, half of the vehicles are outside of the gate and half are inside. Of course with my luck I find myself stuck on the outside. I look around at the traffic of downtown Baghdad. I pull off to the side of the road. I wait—a sacrificial goat tied to a stake—for thirty glassy-eyed minutes, just waiting to be shot at or bombed.

Then we start to move once again, and just down the road another vehicle gets a flat. So I sit for another thirty minutes, and I remember to bend with the wind, to hear the shots, and shouts, and to realize I seldom know the intention of these near and far sounds. So just relax. I have no choice but to just wait. What else can I do? Get mad?

Iraq, 2005

353 Days Remain

We finally began moving again at 0300—three hours to drive out of a fucking gate! Then with lots of little delays along our route I arrived in Mosul around noon—twelve hours to drive a seven-hour route. Now, two days later, I'm on my first actual mission, a patrol through my new home of Mosul. I'm not living on an Iraqi base or even working with Iraqis—yet. I'm living on the big American base called Marez, and today I wander around with other Americans.

The purpose of this patrol is to familiarize myself with the city of Mosul, except I am to do it from the inside of a Stryker vehicle, which is similar to a tank but with wheels. I'm not sure how much "familiarizing" I'm getting, sitting down surrounded by armor. I hear shouts, the occasional warning shot, air horns blaring, and guys screaming "Stop, you fuck, or I'll shoot your head off!" Then I hear an explosion. We swerve and honk and bump across medians, and in the back I sway with the movements; it's hot and I can't see a thing, so I just sweat, and sway.

This patrol I'm on is common here—U.S. soldiers drive throughout the city just to drive, to show a presence, and to be around in case something were to happen, which it inevitably does if you drive around long enough. I hear that the unit I'm on patrol with is good at what they do. Well, I can at least hear them shout and shoot. At what? Hell if I know—but it sounds like they don't take any shit, especially since every car is a possible car bomb, so it's only natural that every car is a dire threat.

"Sir!" a soldier leans down from his perch to yell in my ear. "A vehicle just blew up. We'll be stopped for a while. You want to check out your new home?"

"What the hell," I think, so I unbend from my seat to stand up and take a peek. I see exactly what I expect: there's a charred and smoking car in front of us on a wide but now traffic-less avenue. Soldiers are securing the perimeter, yelling at each other. I try to take in the scene, which reveals my first truth about my new home. Up close, I see the realities of war—a smoking and burning scene straight from the apocalypse, pieces of still-smoking flesh speckled out in a rough semicircle and American soldiers yelling "Take a fucking knee, you fuck! And look out!"—but in the background I see a normal city, with people going to work, walking to school, talking on a cellphone while waiting to cross the road. These Iraqis ignore this spectacle of what is everyday life in Mosul, and I lift my eyes above this landscape to see bushes and trees and rolling hills, which are green, and a sky with just a hint of blue, which is amazing.

"Blew himself up! The second one today," the soldier says, his words pulling me back from my pondering and gazing, and I look to where he points, to the vehicle that now looks like a large bug crushed under a heavy boot. Small flames wink out from the belching black smoke, and within and around us are the smoking remains of the less-than-whole driver and the remnants of a few collateral victims, the pedestrians, who are always present when a bomb goes boom next to an American.

The ramp of the Stryker lowers, and we exit.

"Fucking-A, huh?" The soldier points to the blown-up car. "Check it out," he then says, pointing to a detached penis that's stuck to the side of another Stryker vehicle. I smile, hoping this is from the man who took his own life: a better version of unnatural selection.

"How are things here in Mosul?" I ask.

"Not bad. Things are getting a little better," he says, without looking at me, as we re-enter the Stryker. I sit back down and he returns to his perch. His eyes are always moving, scanning the houses and roads and nearby alleyways. "We're still having a couple of IEDs a day and at least one car bomb per week and, of course, constant small-arms fire. But things are definitely better than before." He quickly raises his M4 to aim at an encroaching vehicle. "Fucking stop, asshole!" he yells and then mutters under his breath: "Damn. Fucker. Want to get shot!? Wait in line like everyone else."

It's now June; but just a few months ago, in November 2004, Mosul was a city completely out of control, a city where the insurgency spilled into the streets. All of the city's police abandoned ship; they just ran away as the insurgents took over. And the only ones left to do anything about it were a Brigade-minus of Army soldiers, some of whom were from Deuce Four, the unit I am driving around with now.

Deuce Four is Army-speak for the 1-24 Infantry Battalion. I've been told that the Battle for Mosul went from street to street, then from house to house, but that Deuce Four quickly retook the city and it's been a hard eight months of ceaseless patrolling and never-ending missions to find and kill insurgents. Now, Coalition forces are back in control, but the city still hides a vibrant and virulent urban insurgency. Iraqi police are back on the job, some Iraqi army soldiers actually patrol, and U.S. soldiers heartily, eagerly thump every insurgent who dares to raise his head. "Good for them," I think. Mosul is definitely not a city you want to fuck around with.

Mosul, which means "linking point" in Arabic, is about three hundred miles northwest of Baghdad and, with close to two million people, is Iraq's third-largest city. Its population is predominantly Arab, but there is a complex tribal, ethnic, and religious stew that includes Kurds, Turkmen, Armenians, and Assyrians, among others. Sunni Muslims are a majority, but there are large numbers of Shi'a Muslims and minorities of Assyrian and Nestorian Christians, Chaldean and Syrian Catholics, Greek Orthodox and Roman Catholics, and Yazeydis. There are many famous dead residents, among them the Old Testament prophet Jonah, who is said to be buried beneath a mosque called *Nebi Yunis*.

It's known for the fabric muslin, and there is a quarry outside the city that still produces beautiful marble. Then there is Mosul University, one of the largest research schools in the Middle East, which is said to be a breeding ground for the insurgency.

"So, what are you going to do here, sir?" yells the Deuce Four soldier. The question is a good one. What am I going to do here?

The U.S. government has finally acknowledged that there is an insurgency, and that if we want to win, training the Iraq Security Forces should become a strategic priority. So the U.S. military hastily created a new organization called the Iraqi Assistance Group, or IAG. The Army scoured every cubicle, nook, cranny, and corner for any breathing soldier, and it even asked the Special Forces to provide a few volunteers. So I raised my hand. I was rushed through some useless training, and now I am here to embed in the Iraqi military and to make them more capable. It's me, they say, who is America's exit strategy, which is sad in a macabre sort of way.

"So, this is Mosul," I think as I return my gaze to the smoke, the shouts, the horns, and the gunshots. For the next year, this is my home: a potpourri of religions, ethnicities, and tribes all seeking revenge for some long-past but not forgotten wrong. This is a city just waiting to boil over.

Germany, September 2011

28 Days Remain

My nose fills with the scent of seared flesh as the sole of my boot touches a softness . . . I open my eyes. I exhale, and then take a deep breath before rolling slowly out of bed, careful not to wake Cheryl or the girls, who are asleep in the room next door. I walk quietly downstairs to begin my daily ritual.

I put water on the stove.

I sit down at the kitchen table.

I close my eyes and rest my head in my hands, and barely move.

I just sit here, waiting.

Slowly, surely, the thoughts come trickling. Soon they become a torrent and I give in. Thoughts run free and instantly take control, and I start my back-and-forth rocking, my thinking, and my quiet below-breath mumbling. Oh God, this completely uncontrollable thinking—no, not thinking, which implies some control, but a bombardment of thoughts. I am going crazy, but I can't accept this admission of weakness. How could this ever happen? I have spent a lifetime confronting problems as challenges, as obstacles to overcome. I reveled in the impossible, most difficult tasks and, until now, it has worked. But not now. Now I am scared, more scared than I have ever been before, because the problem is within me. What's more, it affects more than just me: I have a family.

I rest my elbows on the kitchen table. I take a deep breath and close my eyes . . . for just a second. . . .

Iraq, 2005

349 Days Remain

My familiarization patrol just returned to the American base, and I'm on the one phone we have among eleven people. I'm talking with Amy. As we discuss my two-week Christmas break, which is still months away, the sweat rolls down my face and I tongue the rock dust on the inside of my cheeks and gums. I spit and then lick cracked lips.

Then she says "You don't try. You don't call enough. I spoke with Tim's wife and she says they talk all the time."

Well, I'm with Tim, one of my fellow advisers, every day, and even though his wife says he calls all the time, she's fucking exaggerating. I know. I asked him. Such bullshit. This is the stuff I don't need to deal with. I wish she would realize the pressure these demands put on me.

I tell her I will try to call at least once a week, just like she asks. I know it is important. "It's also important for me to hear your voice," I whisper to an ear a world away, but she doesn't hear, or understand the difficulties involved with a simple phone call. And when I do call, she doesn't talk much—the last time we spoke, the conversation was awkward. I can sense that something is wrong. These fucking concerns follow me through the day and drag me down. I like to hear about the normal, everyday things she's doing. Her voice takes my mind off the worries.

—

I went on patrol again today, and the final destination was one of Saddam's countless palaces.

Coalition forces have taken over these buildings, and now I'm here to use the few computers that sit in a small room at the top of a winding marble staircase. I look up to see thirty-foot ceilings and beautiful crystal chandeliers. Lining the walls of the main entranceway are twenty-foot tile frescoes of a smiling Saddam Hussein—Saddam lying on his back holding a playful child on his lap and a comforting hand on this youthful head. On another wall is another idyllic scene of Saddam, the caring leader, who stands towering over a veiled and shrunken grandmother. Saddam's hand rests on her head as she looks up in wonder and respect. These scenes litter so many buildings, they feel almost religious in nature, and they are all disturbing. I ask my interpreter to pose for a picture beside one of these frescoes. He is Kurdish and tells me "Hell, no." His memories of oppression and torture and subjugation are real and recent; to him these frescoes mean something very different. As I look over the hundreds of colors and see them combine to tell a story, I think about the mural I now create.

I've been in Iraq for only weeks, and tomorrow I leave the American base of Marez. Tomorrow I make the move to start my life on the Iraqi base. Tomorrow I start a new life in a new place that Saddam Hussein once called the Guest House.

There are stories of how Saddam's sons used my soon-to-be new home. It's unsettling to think of the things that happened in the buildings, perhaps in the same room, where I will sleep.

The other day I took a short trip to visit the place where I will soon live.

The Guest House is run-down: waterless fountains, overgrown rose bushes, empty pools filled with razor wire. We hope to hire some local citizens to bring back the beauty of the grounds, doing our small part to stimulate the local economy. "Small steps," I think, as I stare at the computer where I finish my letter to Amy. I hit SEND and then begin a second letter to my parents, which brings on a smile.

They are such wonderful people and parents—I'm the product of a lifetime of their love and care. I was raised, I rebelled, and I failed and excelled, all in a home of unconditional love and support. Yes, expectations were high, standards were fair and consistently enforced, but love and praise were generously given. Time gives me perspective, and now I see that my parents' central theme was to "make a difference." I have grown up as a witness to how they have lived according to their own philosophy as well. They were once in the Peace Corps, and I have chosen a career that seems the opposite of theirs. But is it really? I guess the metric comes down to intent, which determines the right or wrong of every human thing. As I sit here in Iraq and prepare for a year on a small Iraqi base, I know my intentions are good. I hope my actions will make my parents proud. I hope I'll also make a difference in the world.

Germany, September 2011

27 Days Remain

Open palms come first. The stinging cables are for later . . . I take a breath, the same breath that I took yesterday morning, and then the morning before that . . . *the pain is unbearable . . .* just one breath, one more than the day before . . . my heart beats faster. . . .

. . . my eyes open. I press fingers into my temples and rotate my elbows forward to keep my eyes hidden.

I have been feeling this way for three days now; hundreds of unconnected thoughts ricochet inside my head, and I desperately try to link them together. They are an uncontrollable rush; but then out from the chaos flies a tidbit of sanity. I furiously scribble it down: a morsel that I'm terrified of forgetting. Funny, my thoughts have never been this important to me before, until last week, that is, and these thoughts that jump back and forth between the past and present feel especially important this morning as I sit at the kitchen table: my thinking begins to coalesce on my fading marriage. . . .

I want us to work, and I have tried so very hard for such a long time. But slowly, over the years, I've come to realize that I'm just not the same man as before. Now I'm impatient, angry, and judgmental. I try, every day, to be someone different, but my trying doesn't make things better; my "trying" doesn't matter. Marriage counseling? It wasn't getting at the root of the problem: the counselors didn't care about understanding, they cared only about applying ointment to the scars. Nothing worked. But things have to improve. They have to, because I am driving us apart, and our problems are really my problems. And what *am* I? I feel insubstantial, ephemeral; only a reflection of an echo who can't reach out to what is essential, Cheryl and the girls, my three angels.

I know. I know that their absence would be unbearable. I would stumble and fall in that world. I wouldn't want to continue.

Iraq, 2005

342 Days Remain

I've been at the Guest House for over a week now, and my Iraqi counterpart, Saedi, just arrived a few mornings ago.

He came with a group of forty Iraqis to look over his new home, and to meet his American adviser. Me.

Most of the Iraqis he came with were officers, and my guess is they want to have first pick of the best rooms before their soldiers arrive.

There is only one large building on this small Iraqi base. So the Iraqis swarm over this three-story structure, and most climb up the stairs to pick over the best choices. But my guy? He goes spiraling down to the basement and picks out six dark and mildewed rooms in the farthest back corner, away from all peeking and prying eyes.

As I tour the building with Saedi, I feel all the past horrors in these hidden places, but he doesn't care, or waste a second getting down to business. These basement rooms are a perfect makeshift prison. But my tour with Saedi took place two days ago, and a lot has happened since then. Now, there are insurgents in our little prison, and Saedi has been at them for a day now. And tonight I will take part in the interrogations. Tonight is my first night in a cell, and I know tonight I will need my rest, so I take a nap and wake up around midnight.

I slip quietly out of my room, which is in the building next door. I'm careful not to wake my roommate; but when I exit my building, I hurry the one hundred feet to enter through the Iraqi building's front door. Iraqis are on guard, talking, smoking, and drinking tea. I smile and they smile back, and then things really start to get dark. Power is sparse in Iraq and especially on this Iraqi base. Light bulbs are only for key offices, so hallways and stairwells are often pitch-black.

There are two windows in the stairwell that descends to the basement, so on cloudless nights the moonlight lends me a hand. I descend and wind to the left with my arms extended to the sides. As I step off the bottom step to land on the basement floor, I sense a transition. Brown mildew stews on the walls. I can't see these brown stains, but I know they are there, growing. I begin walking forward, and then I see a small light coming from a distant room far down to the right. I move slowly, and then I turn right to enter into Saedi's bedroom, which also doubles as his office.

Saedi is seated, leaning back, with a lighted cigarette in one hand; in the other are prayer beads, constantly moving between thumb and forefinger. A cell phone rests between a bent head and raised shoulder and, of course, there, reverently centered on the wall right behind this Kurdish Iraqi Army officer, is the smiling face of Massoud Barzani, the son of the even more revered Kurdish legend, Mustafa Barzani.

As I enter, I give him a respectful slight nod, and then I notice his cot on the left. It sags in the middle and every metal post corner has something hanging from it: an AK-47, a camouflage shirt, an old leather pistol holster, some grungy off-white butt-hugging underwear. His bed is unmade, with a rough wool red blanket wadded up at the foot. His desk is to the right as I enter his door.

It is sparse and all business: a nothing-fancy, plain metal rectangle with the omnipresent pistol, three cell phones, a smoking and overflowing glass ashtray, a notepad, a fancy pen, and a gold-gilded small teacup in the middle.

I sit down and we pass pleasantries.

I say "Salaam Alaikum, Saedi" and then, in English that is translated into Arabic, I continue: "It is so good to see you. So, who are you talking with tonight?" That's a Kurdish freedom-fighter euphemism for "Which prisoner will you break?"

He responds in Arabic, which is quickly translated into English by the interpreter seated to my right. He gives me the names of a prisoner or two, and we then discuss the day's totals of suspected terrorists taken in and those he will be forced to set free.

"Why are they set free?" I ask.

"I pressure them for sometimes hours, sometimes days," he says. "Make them miserable and find they are innocent or didn't confess, you see?"

Saedi and I idly finish our required small talk—and business dealings—and then we rise and move slowly to the other dark rooms down at the end of the basement hall, to the rooms that have become a makeshift prison. Today, there are several terrorists held in six prison cells, cells that are half-heartedly constructed with cinderblock walls, each with a metal door that is locked by the small twist of a flimsy metal tie. Two uncovered light bulbs hang limply from opposing ends of the prison and spread a dreary absence of natural light. The rooms are cold, quiet, and slightly damp. And then we talk about who are new guests to the Guest House.

"Ryhad came to conduct a recon on our base at 10:30 last night," says Saedi. "The guards found him hiding in the grass. His leader's name was Sharabe. When we captured Ryhad, I knew he was a terrorist. How? When I inspected his wallet, I found only 250 Iraqi dinar; at 10:30 at night with no money? What is he doing here? This person is the weak point in a cell, the worker, and we captured him last night."

Saedi takes a quick puff from his cigarette, waits a few seconds enjoying the buzz, and then he continues. "I told Ryhad, 'I know you came here to attack us.'

"We did not let him sleep all night. We keep him confused . . . telling him to 'get up, to go, to come back' with his hands tied to his back and with a sandbag on his head. I told him, 'Listen, it is useless for you to deny. If you deny, we will execute you' and we started to take him out back. He started crying, and I then told him 'We know that you are a poor man and that they forced you to do this job. If you deny, we will execute you. If you confess, we will help you. If you talk about your cell and tell us all, you will be released in four months because you are a poor man.'

"All of this was not true, of course," says Saedi, "but just to make him afraid, and to have hope. He began to confess about putting IEDs on roads and firing mortars, and he gave us a lot of information about his cell."

This is all in Arabic, of course, so the conversation takes a long, long time.

Saedi takes another breath, quickly pulls his cigarette to his mouth, and then continues.

"Yesterday morning Ryhad led us to Mahmoud and his two brothers. And then we had Ryhad confront Mahmoud, who then confessed and then Mahmoud led us to Ismael, Ibrahim, and three other cell members. That was yesterday afternoon. And then we had Ryhad and Mahmoud confront these terrorists with their accusations, and these new prisoners led us to Gazim, Haji and his two sons. We put them all together in the large room next door. They began arguing, and cursing, and telling on each other, and then we acted quickly and tonight we captured the entire twelve-man terrorist cell. It was a busy day."

I nod and exclaim amazement at his interrogation prowess, and in reality I am amazed. I am learning a fine art from a practicing master, a Kurdish Peshmerga, an intelligence officer in the Asayesh, the notorious Kurdish Intelligence Service, and now a colonel in the new Iraqi Army, three decades of this work and in that order. In other words, he is freakish good at getting people to say things they don't want to.

I wonder to myself, "Why is he so good?" But then I realize this isn't such a mystery. His skills are the same as those used everywhere in the world. Saedi knows what questions to ask, how to ask them, and how to manipulate the prisoner to intentionally or unintentionally respond. He has mastered the art of the Approach, and his Approach is based on his thorough knowledge of the prisoner: his language, religion, culture, geographical region, neighborhood, family, friends, lovers, associates, and secret routines. And, of course, there is the "pressure," the abuse which is the cherry on the top of ice cream. And for the self-righteous who say making terrorists suffer is wrong, and who are concerned about the chance prisoner who turns out to be innocent? "Well, fuck it," my government and I'd respond with indignation: After 9/11, Human Rights don't apply to killers of Americans, and the remote chance of hurting an innocent is the hard but necessary price of our war against terrorism.

So, yes, Saedi is a master. When he enters a cell, he looks into the mind and heart of a killer and can say to himself, "I know you and understand why you kill." This is what I must become to be just as successful.

And when the guards slowly raise the sandbag from a prisoner's head and his scared and weary eyes begin to focus, the first thing he sees through the cigarette smoke is Saedi's thick mustache hanging beneath jet-black eyes. When this happens, killers turn to panic and most start to cry, for they realize that this time, they aren't prisoners of the soft Americans.

Germany, September 2011

26 Days Remain

How could I subject my wife and children to this? But asking "how" implies choice. I am not choosing this. It's 3:30 A.M. again.

I want my children to grow up surrounded by the love of two parents who love each other. Yet I am consumed by anger. I am unsociable, disagreeable, and temperamental. I am impatient. Yet I have an amazing wife and two perfect girls, whom I love and who love me. Why can't I just deal with this, this weakness? Why can't I change? How is that possible?

Cheryl married me, she loves me, and so she must see through me; she must see the man who is in hiding. And that man? Somewhere deep down he knows that she is all that he's missing, all that he is not.

She is empathetic, selfless, emotional, silly, and funny. She is patient, impressionable, non-judgmental. She is sociable, talkative, and friendly, and has intimate friends whom she loves and who love her. She spends lots of time with her family, and even believes in God, for fuck's sake.

We are so different, but I know with absolute clarity that I desperately need her. But what if I can't stop this continual slide into a past that won't say good-bye? How much more of me can she take?

Germany, September 2011

26 Days Remain

And who is this new me?

I speak, I judge, I hurt. And then I argue. This argument leads to another misunderstanding that hurts, and then we argue about that second misunderstanding, then we miscommunicate; I judge again, we hurt some more. The argument repeats, and then escalates. I think that I calmly, rationally, and persistently explain what she did wrong and why I was upset, but not angry. She doesn't understand; and even if she could understand my explanation, she now cannot even remember how the argument began. She closes her eyes and gives up; I continue to talk. She gets overwhelmed by my reasoning, by my "energy," and then she gets really, really, mad. A look of disgust suddenly transforms her angelic face.

I am now hurt, not just upset. But mostly, painfully, I am sad that I am the cause of a disagreement between two people in love that produces an emotion close to hate. I am hurt that I am changed and I can't seem to change. She senses my sadness and feels that I am intentionally trying to inflict guilt. I need comfort. She feels forced to act in a way she does not feel. I withdraw. She doesn't follow. I love her so much, I'm desperate to repair what I damaged before it's too late, and we fall exhausted to sleep. But we can't seem to start fresh, to forgive, then to forget. She just wants me to stop.

So I give up. We fall asleep, Cheryl in the bed and me on the couch.

In the morning, the echoes of lost love bounce off the walls and I try hard to pretend to go on. I can't forget, but I still love her with the same intensity I felt on the day we were married; her love for me is always one notch less. Soon there will be nothing left and I will be hanging by a hair, by an unraveling, stretching thread, only seconds away from the final tear. God, I don't want to fall. I have to fix this.

Were the few smiles and many horrors over this last decade of war for some greater purpose? It helps to think so, sometimes, but I can't help thinking I've failed some cosmic test; I'm in purgatory, a living and breathing million moments of missing. Am I meant to be forever in distress?

I stand up from the kitchen table.

I glance at the microwave clock: 4 A.M.

It's been an hour since I came downstairs.

I am still thinking and thinking, and I know I need to move.

So I walk to the bathroom and stand and then creep left toward the mirror. One ear, then one cheek—I tilt my head just a bit to the left. I see an eye and then I take a peek. What will I see? I never know, even when I see that it is just me.

"What is unhappiness?" I ask the reflection. "It's emotion using reason to understand this world," responds the apparition.

Iraq, 2005

324 Days Remain

Six more prisoners came in last night, so I walk over to Saedi's room to do a surprise inspection. Of course, I don't phrase it this way. Hopefully, he'll just think I'm being social.

On my way over to say hello, I force a smile and pull the string that makes me say "Salaam Alaikum" to a group of Iraqi soldiers. They are squatting and talking in a circle, and behind these squatting and talking soldiers are other Iraqis who are marching; brown boots and old camouflage uniform tops stand with arms and legs straight. They begin moving, back and forth, up and down their arms go, and a hundred feet start making uneven stomping sounds. This place, this culture, these people, and these soldiers, are so different, so unlike anything I know.

I wave at the Iraqi Gestapo as I enter Saedi's building. I descend the stairs to the basement, and I make a beeline to his office door, and I enter and say "Saedi. Kaifa haluka? How are you?"

He holds up two fingers to say he will be a few minutes more as he talks on his mobile phone. He finishes the call and then the other phone rings. So I wait a few minutes more, stirring my chai and looking at the few pictures on the wall.

"Alaikum Salaam. Do you want some tea?" he asks as he hangs up the phone. I raise the glass that is already full. "La Shukran. No, thank you."

"Some new prisoners arrived last night. Would you like to see?" he asks.

"Na'am, Saedi. Please." I smile.

Saedi and I slowly walk to the quiet cells to take a peek. I look inside. There are no beds, no chairs, no table, no light, and no place to take a leak. So a few times a day the Iraqi guards take them outside to a porta-john, which we have provided. The Iraqis are not trying to be cruel; they just don't have the money for such unnecessary luxuries.

Despite the poor conditions, I sense they are trying to take care of these men. Actually, I think they are cared for more than they deserve. They make sure they have enough water, are properly fed, are not cold, and they ask for an American when one of them gets sick. So, they do care for these prisoners. But the "caring" is for a purpose.

Here, kindness is just another technique, a tactic to use for the interrogation, and Saedi knows the perfect circumstances in which to take it away. And it works. They are nice, then mean, then angry, then happy, then hit and slap and hurt and scare; they laugh and then show regret and sadness and then share stories and then go quiet. But these emotions are all just masks, just good interrogation. Getting killers to confess requires a complete range of skills, and emotions called up on cue is an important one. But for some reason, this charade is difficult. I only feel hate toward these terrorists. Hate is not the range I'm used to. I will just start faking all the other emotions required of me and, maybe, one day, the masquerade will come.

I ask the guard to open each door that we pass; there are six doors to six cells, but often we have many more than just six prisoners.

"Why the sandbags?" I ask as I look in the first room.

"Sandbags have several goals," says Saedi. "So the interrogator and place of interrogation is not identified, and also to make their minds imagine. Imagination is much worse than reality. Here, their mind is their worst enemy. Also, I don't want them to form an impression of the interrogator, of me, so they cannot form opinions of the interrogator's strengths, weaknesses, or intelligence. What they imagine I will do is much worse than anything I can possibly do."

"Who is the next one?" I ask as we move down to the cell next door.

"This is Rashid. Rashid has barely talked; he seems strong. We inspected his cell phone. In his phone was a picture of his nephew, who looks about five months old." As we enter Rashid's cell, Saedi squats down and says, in a soft voice filled with compassion, "Rashid, do you know what we just found out? Your nephew has a bad disease and he is right now in the hospital with oxygen on his face. I hear he may die." Saedi places a hand on Rashid's shoulder and does a compassionate squeeze.

"Please, let me see him one time before he dies," Rashid pleads.

"No!" Saedi yells, and then in quiet mock sympathy his leans into an ear and says, "He will die and you will be here and you will miss the ceremony and only females will bury him. If you want to see your nephew, you will speak with us."

"Let's leave him to think," whispers Saedi after we exit the cell and close the door. "Sometimes you find that one single thing that will break them. Most of the time, you never know what it is, but in time it will come, it always does. Just have patience. But if this takes too long? You learn other methods when this one fails; sometimes we use a relative. Telling a terrorist that you will bring in a wife or child is a good method. This was often done under Saddam, and the people understand and expect that this will happen. If a person is not married, then we say we will bring his mother. Terrorists always want to see their mommy before they die."

"And what about him?" I ask as we move to the next cell.

"His name is Radwan. He came in two nights ago and we confronted him with facts. We faced Radwan with so many facts, and we did not react to his excuses or denials. He claims his brother was accidentally killed by a stray round from a fight between terrorists and the Iraqi police. But we know differently. We confronted him with the real reason behind his brother's death. His brother was killed when he attacked some American Strykers; we confronted him with a large amount of details about his operations, his associations, his neighborhood, his family. Radwan had limits, so a combination of continual bombardment of facts, denial of cigarettes, and we gave him lots of water and did not allow him to use the restroom. For the whole night we made him sit down, then stand up, and then sit down. We pushed him, we pressed him, and we faced him some more. We made him stand out in the cold. Finally, Radwan started to cry and I knew he was ready.

"The most important person in the interrogation of Radwan was Nyah, who is an informant from Radwan's neighborhood. Nyah was present during the interrogation yesterday. He wore a mask, an Iraqi uniform, and pretended to assist with notes. Having an informant in the interrogation is a very good technique. That way we can instantly check his answers, and this way it seems as if we know everything. All of the interrogation assistants wear masks—mostly for security reasons—but because of this, when we put an informant within the interrogation room this technique is not suspected. Radwan rightfully believed that there was a person very close to him who was working with us. Radwan was overwhelmed. He thought we knew everything!" Saedi chuckles, and then pulls the cigarette to his mouth.

"And him?" I ask at the next door, pointing to a man lying down on the cold floor.

"He has done several assassinations and kidnappings. We asked him to swear an oath on the Koran, to Allah, to the Prophet

Mohammed—'alayhi as-salām—to swear that he did not rape and kill a girl. You remember, the same girl whose father came here the other night, the father who was crying and who asked us to help find his little girl?

"This oath we had this killer take is considered a very important questioning technique. If it does not get a detainee to break, then it will definitely cause him a mental struggle. This is important to begin the process of breaking his resistance. However, this does not work on a Salafi Takfiri. Remember, they have been taught and they believe that we are unbelievers because we are supporting unbelievers, so swearing falsely is allowed and will be forgiven by Allah."

"And him?" I ask before we enter the last cell.

"There are two terrorists in this cell. One is a sniper. I found out that he may be gay. I brought in a man and told him he was a doctor. The 'doctor' brought in his tools, stripped him, and checked him, and we told him we'd put this information on the television. This broke him, so we brought him to our office and gave him drinks and cookies, and he talked and talked."

"And the other guy?" I ask.

"Adultery," responds Saedi. "We told him we would tell his family. He cried and admitted to emplacing IEDs."

"I don't know about America," he says when we go back to his office, "but in Iraq, public accusation of cheating, or having sex with men, is worse than terrorism."

Germany, September 2011

24 Days Remain

The changing in my brain hurts, but still I force myself to get up and go to work. Later in the day I drive across Germany to give some important briefings at Landstuhl Regional Medical Center. During these meetings I am completely clear-minded, able to say the thoughts that are in my head with abnormal precision and confidence. I am sociable and extemporaneous, and during the second briefing I sit down with some high-ranking and important people—not important because of their rank but because of their profession and the larger group of people this small group represents.

For soldiers deployed to Iraq and Afghanistan, the men and women at Landstuhl are like guardian angels who stand ready. We know it's coming and that their arms stretch out to wait patiently—so many dying soldiers rushed through these doors to this place where hundreds of lives are dedicated to saving life.

And then my briefing ends and I tell the assembled audience: "I have something personal I would like to say. I want to express my sincere gratitude for you and for all that you do. I have always wanted to come here but have never had the opportunity until now, so I now want to say thank you." And then I completely lose control.

I start to cry and my body shakes, and I can't stop. I try to stop, to pull back the tears and to pretend with a smile that nothing happened. But I can't. I have no control of myself.

I give a professional briefing to a small group of high-ranking Army officers, and I cry? Some colleagues of mine show alarm and ask if I'm okay, but I brush it off as nothing of concern, just a momentary lapse. But in truth I'm scared. I'm cracking.

I get in the car and rush home, terrified, and during the long drive my thoughts and memories start to take control and push away the reality of the road in front of me. I pull the car over and stare, and behind my eyes I return to Washington, D.C., pulled back to my first week home from Iraq, to May 2006 . . . to the hateful traffic, horns, and rushing citizens who live with their heads down, blind and oblivious to the others who do their bidding, who do their dying. . . .

Iraq, 2005

323 Days Remain

I stand on the perimeter of the Guest House and watch through razor wire as the Tigris River flows by, as a depressing moon rises over rooftops, and its glow pushes through columns of black smoke in the distance. I unconsciously tilt my head into the wind's caress as my thoughts turn to Amy.

Our lives are so distant, and so vastly different.

Right now she is on holiday break with friends and family, sitting in the back yard grilling salmon. She writes when she has time. Meanwhile, I've returned from a patrol to begin an interrogation of a terrorist, and after two hours of convincing I now just stand and stare through the razor wire. My gaze falls on the far riverbank. I hear the sound of gunfire and reflect on another night of fitful sleep: the power is out—again—and it's so fucking hot that sweat flows to drench my face and neck, then trickles down my back. I reach up to wipe my brow with the sleeve of a stretched-out brown T-shirt, and my eyes return to see the outline of feeding water buffalo.

I often find myself standing beside this river, and occasionally I play a game with myself: I shut my mind to what surrounds me, to travel slowly to a place that my mind creates. When I push reality into the background, I can imagine amazingly beautiful landscapes empty of people.

As the hot breeze blows across this riverbank, I look up to see the shaking branches and waving leaves and I hear them making peaceful rustling noises until they break and slowly fall. I am transfixed by the moonlight that reflects off flowing river water; I can actually hear the water slide over the riverbanks and I imagine myself standing on a shoreline in San Luis Obispo, where I went to university and was commissioned an Infantry second lieutenant. I miss San Luis Obispo and running the trails of Montaña de Oro that overlook sand dunes and tidal pools.

Now, years later, I live in a place called Nineveh Province and my place in this world is put back into perspective. Every direction I look, every hilltop I stand on, and every valley I traverse, I imagine the thousands of centuries where countless feet stepped before me. Whole civilizations have come and gone, over and over, and I am awed by my insignificance.

While driving the outer boundary of my area today, I passed the Nebi Yunis mosque. Only two kilometers east from where I now stand is this ancient building with its minaret rising. This spire watches over what is said to be the final resting place of the Old Testament prophet Jonah. As I try to find the outline of this mosque in the moonlight, I think of the history, the sheer span of time that surrounds me, and this small feeling is comforting.

The city is quiet at this time of night. There is still the occasional sound of gunfire and sometimes an explosion, but overall the city slowly becomes silent after dark. This is when Iraqis slowly emerge to their rooftops to savor the relative coolness of the night and to then fall slowly asleep. It's as if night is a time when all honor an unspoken ceasefire.

I look down at my wristwatch—it's time. I turn away from the Tigris and leave the razor wire to get ready for our night patrol.

Curfew starts at 2300, so we start moving at 2315. We drive the city streets at night, and at this late dark hour the streets are empty. Tonight the battleground is silent, and you can almost imagine that not a single soul lived. Which is why area familiarization is better at night; for a variety of reasons, nocturnal the terrorists are not. First, their camouflage and prey—the Iraqi civilian—sleeps at night. If they were to show themselves at this dark hour, with our technology and training it would be easier for us to find and kill them. Second, terrorists are fucking lazy. I think of the potential of these killers if they were to show a little more industry beyond their complete disregard for life and their eagerness to die for a hateful god.

I drive through the night, and the hot winds blow hard with trash and sand and dust flying through the air, and I can only see about a hundred feet in front of the vehicles, even when using our portable spotlight. The gunner in the turret operates the light, and with this small moving circle we scan the streets and side alleyways. Periodically the beam of light startles a scavenging dog, the only life.

A new day begins and I need to clear my head, so this morning I force myself to get up and jog two and a half miles around the Guest House. Thank God for these morning runs, on the few mornings when I actually do drag myself up and out at 6 A.M. This morning it is beautiful outside, although "beautiful" is relative.

At the beginning of the Iraq war, this base was the home of a U.S. Army Battalion, I think from the 101st Airborne Division. But it was soon turned back to the Iraqi government. Now, after six months of Iraqi Army use and abuse, it is dirty beyond description. But things are a little better and getting slightly cleaner. When I arrived here, the hallways and storerooms, just about any room, had been used as a bathroom. Trash was dropped where one stood, where one sat or slept, and piles of trash had gathered everywhere. Complete building floors went unused because people lived in a room until their presence made it unlivable, and then they moved to another room where this process repeated again. On the other hand, I'm learning that the Iraqis are friendly and infinitely curious.

I went to our tiny little weight room this morning and an Iraqi *jundee*—Arabic for an Army private—saw that I was working out and came in, sat and watched, and watched, and watched. He tried to communicate by hand sign, by flexing his small bicep muscles, and he thought if he just talked to me in Arabic slower and louder I would soon understand. If I lifted a weight, he would pick up a larger one. He would grunt and groan and smile. I smiled in return. And he would then grunt and groan louder, responding to my encouragement.

After my indoor weight training, I go outside to stretch. The sky is clear and the morning is blessedly silent; and when finished with my workout, I go up to my rooftop to give Amy a call. It's nice to hear her talk about wine, a movie, and my head on her lap. I miss these things terribly, and this morning I feel the need for this comfort more profoundly than usual.

Then she says "Why haven't you sent a present yet?" She wants me to search the Souks to find her something uniquely Iraqi.

Doesn't she understand?

I live in a combat zone. I only drive around if we are doing an operation, either with Iraqis or by ourselves. I don't simply cruise around shopping. Does she understand this?

When I leave the base I am on patrol, with all of my armor and weapons, doing an operation, looking for vehicle bombs, for hidden weapons, searching homes and shops. I am in the blistering sun, walking or driving, head constantly turning, senses over-loaded trying to find anything out of place, a person getting too close, wearing too much clothing, a vehicle that is speeding and weighed down, a person on a rooftop, a bomb planted someplace that hopefully you can see before its penetrating charge slices through the side door of your pathetically armored right-angled vehicle. I am blistering with heavy gear covering my body in 110-degree heat, my radio earphones cover my ears under my helmet, and there is a constant buzz of talk. My feet are swollen, and sweat runs into my eyes and soaks my shirt, as my head and eyes are moving up, down, to the sides, behind me, taking in and processing the movements of hundreds of people and vehicles in a bustling city of millions with traffic and pedestrians moving in all directions, knowing that at any second it could be my last second.

Fuck! There is no getting out and exploring and shopping for a girlfriend who wants trinkets! I know these times are hard and I should try harder to remember all the things she does for me, but she is suspicious when I stay silent. She asks "Why are you so distant? Why are you not calling? Is there someone else?"

For fuck's sake! Our lives are so fucking far apart. I wish I could respond to her complaints with a small dose of my reality, the daily dance with death and then the interrogation of killers.

She has every day, every night, every new friend, thousands of new experiences, all of which could lead to someone new, and with me only a vanishing memory, someone she loves but whose face soon fades to become an indistinct, out-of-focus, distant memory. The days become weeks, and weeks turn to months, and these months will soon become a year; over time she suddenly becomes aware that the love she once felt has . . . disappeared.

Tomorrow will be 117 degrees, and I still have no air conditioning, so sweat drips and drips, and with each drip I become one drop less.

Germany, September 2011

24 Days Remain

Despite my stop on the side of the road, the return drive from Landstuhl is finally over and I'm parked outside of my house . . . I'm home? How long have I been sitting here in the driveway, just staring at the windshield?

I open the car door and walk through my front door. I take off my shoes and head up the stairs to immediately pour myself a drink—a drink that I both hate and desperately need. Later, Cheryl and I sing the girls to sleep, then sit down to watch a movie, but tonight I don't just hear what the actors are saying: for some reason, I am overwhelmed by the emotions they are play-acting.

⌐

SATINE: I'm sorry, Christian, I'm dying.
CHRISTIAN: No, you'll be all right.
SATINE: I'm so sorry, Christian. I'm sorry. I'm cold. Hold me. You've got to carry on without me, Christian.

CHRISTIAN: I can't carry on without you.

SATINE: You have so much to give.

CHRISTIAN: No.

SATINE: Tell our story, Christian.

CHRISTIAN: I love you.

SATINE: Tell our story, Christian, that way I'll always be with you.

CHRISTIAN: (typing): Days turned into weeks, weeks turned into months, and then on a not-so very special day, I sat down at my typewriter and I wrote down our story. A story about a time, a story about a place, a story about the people. But most importantly, a story about love. A love that will live forever. The end.

And I cry.

Lately, I feel something more than nothing. I go from angry to being high, and I'm happy, or maybe ecstatic, which is amazing because I haven't felt this way for a long, long time; since Iraq, it seems. And that's a long time—five years I've felt an absence, and I've never noticed this before? Is this what other people feel? Is this what I've been missing? Looking back, I guess I got so used to feeling nothing that this "absence" just became me. But now every feeling is coming back, suddenly—gray has transformed into a million-hued charging elephant—and I don't know if I can take it. It's overwhelming. I feel flash-frozen. Hold me just a fraction of an inch above the ground, then just let go.

And then I hear a CRACK; I look down and see red wine, blood, and splinters of glass everywhere, and realize I had been holding my wine glass, holding it tighter and tighter without realizing the pressure was becoming too much for the glass to bear. I glance at Cheryl, and she looks scared.

Iraq, 2005

318 Days Remain

It is 2 A.M. as I walk from my room to the entrance of Saedi's building. The morning is dark; there is no moon and the clouds block every star.

I usually stand outside for a little while before I enter his building. I enjoy the stillness and the silence, the fleeting rays of moon and starlight. But this morning I decide to just walk quickly across the wet grass and cold cement; there is no solace in this morning's dark. But this is not the same for Saedi. Here, the absence of light seems to offer him some degree of comfort, so maybe it is just my perspective that needs altering.

As I enter the office, Saedi takes a slow drag from his cigarette and then nonchalantly waves a hand toward a vacant seat. Ah, my seat: the metal folding chair that waits near the opposite side of the room. It's always waiting. It's never-changing. Day after day, week after week; thousands of times my ass drops into that seat, which is always empty, just waiting for me. It's crazy, but the damn thing seems sentient. That seat seems to know what I want, what I need, how I feel. I sit.

My interpreter sits on the bed behind me. I never sit on the bed. I just don't ever want to plop down on the place where Saedi sleeps, even though everyone else seems at ease with this. To me, this seems presumptuous, invasive, and a little dirty.

So I wait for him to end a phone call and to then begin the mandatory small talk. I wait, in silence, and think on the smoke that surrounds me. I can't stand all the smoke in these rooms and the incessant smoking of everyone I interact with, but I tell myself that I have no choice, so just endure, keep your hands and mind busy, hold on to the glass of sweet chai. Just stir, take false sips, and stir, and then take a few sips more. My mind wanders during these endless minutes of waiting.

Today I ponder the prison cells that are just a few rooms down from this room's door. Will today bring us a thief, a rapist, or a killer? Sometimes I like to think about what movie I will watch before I go to bed. Or I silently mouth a few new Arabic words I've learned. Or I wonder if I will find chicken, lamb, or fish in tonight's stew. Is there a car bomb, right now, roving around this base, waiting to rush the gates? How about my friendly neighborhood sniper or mortar men? Or maybe the simple act of a terrorist climbing our fence undetected and wearing a suicide vest. And why don't the prisoners ever make noise?

I never hear our prisoners make noise. I haven't thought of this before and I now wonder why. It's not as if they can't talk. They talk all the time . . . they blah-blah all the time about what they did or what they swear to God they didn't do, but when we leave the cell they go silent.

"Saedi," I ask from the chair at the corner of his bed, "you always seem to get prisoners to talk. How?" I wait a handful of seconds for the interpreter to turn my English into Arabic. The seconds seem endless.

"These are our people," he answers, "and we know them better than you. Sources and detainees give information; we are able to check the information."

Saedi's English is awful, as is my Arabic, so our conversations are long and painful. But we both need each other, so we endure the endless time it takes to complete a thought.

I ask again, hoping for more detail: "But how do you get these prisoners to talk, even when they don't want to?"

"A special way," he responds. "I cannot tell you."

I then realize he is not yet ready to divulge his behind-closed-door secrets—but then he decides to continue with what I can tell is less than the whole truth. He doesn't fully trust me.

"Mr. Bill, I will tell a terrorist that I captured another one of his group. 'And now I have information about you,' I will tell them. 'I know you are a poor man and that somebody forced you to do these horrible actions.'

"You remember Abbas Kannas, Mr. Bill? The terrorist who was here last week who we think killed some Americans? He did not confess after three days! Informants told us that Abbas's leader is Shaeb. Well, I forced Abbas to drink lots of water and didn't allow him to pee. I didn't let him sleep, and then we tell him, 'We know you are really the sniper Kanas. You must speak with us. If you do, we will not beat you. We have captured your leader Shaeb, so we know everything! Everything! You will speak with us. He has said you are involved with this attack on Americans. We captured one of your brothers and his kids. If you speak, we will release your brother and his children.'

"And then, Mr. Bill, I allow the interrogation room to go quiet, and the silence is as sharp as a weapon. He then confessed! Why did he confess?" Saedi asks rhetorically. "Because we lied to him, we gave him water and then didn't allow him to pee. We made him stand naked in the cold for hours. We made him squat with his back against a wall. We kept the lights on. We didn't let him sleep. We gave him no peace. Because of these things and because of the false capture of his leader and the false capture of his brother and children, this is why he confessed. They think we know everything so that it is hopeless to resist. Their only hope is my leniency, my mercy, so he thinks confessing will make me go soft on him."

Saedi understands these insurgents. Is it even possible for me to get to them the way he does? Probably not, but I will do my best. After all, I have many months to learn, and over dozens of interrogations I have already learned so much. I am beginning to see some things more clearly—like why Saedi is successful at getting people to talk.

He is successful because he is able to answer these questions: Why is this prisoner a terrorist? Who supports and sustains them and why? What is the purpose of this group or cell? Why do they fight? How are these groups and cells led and organized and interconnected?

"Whenever I have information about someone already," Saedi tells me, "before we capture him, this information we have is very important. We call this 'primary information.' If we do not have primary info, I will call our sources and neighborhood contacts and ask for information, and if this does not work, we will ask you to check to see if there is American Intelligence."

Saedi tells me that this is how he forms his important "first questions." And by knowing the answers he is able to establish the foundation of his interrogation: the atmospherics, the approach, the questioning plan. Later, this primary information helps him to identify the prisoner's resistance techniques, which then allow him to further refine his next step. This is the interrogation. But what else has he taught me? He knows that most terrorists are really just common criminals we have relabeled and that these men never act from a single motivation. In reality, there are usually many reasons why someone resorts to acts of terror and this combination of motivations is what drives each man. The interaction of many motivations creates weak points within a person. These "fractures" are what he identifies and then exploits. If a person is an insurgent because he is poor and his son is sick, this knowledge provides Saedi a thousand different levers to pry out words from behind clenched teeth.

I am starting to get better at this. I must become an expert on the personal details of each individual. I must be an expert on the topic under discussion: on the history of Iraq, the dynamics of insurgency, and especially on the dynamics of this unique Iraqi Insurgency. I must be an expert at mentally categorizing each detainee: determine as precisely as possible their motivations for becoming an insurgent and what type of insurgent they are. Is this insurgent poor, uneducated, unintelligent, and simple, without a job, immature and religiously lost? Or is he a member of a hardened criminal gang who takes advantage of the instability caused by no security? Is this prisoner very religious, someone who believes that it is his obligation as a devout Muslim to kill non-believers and anyone else who supports them? Is this prisoner a rich man who is threatened? Is he a former Baathist who is seeking a return to a glorious past, to the day he once held a position of power and prestige? Is he just a nationalist? Is he *actually* innocent? These are just a fraction of the many questions I must answer, and the more confident I am of each answer, the more assured I become of the approach I must use. Only then can I ever enter a cell to interrogate these men.

And this mental classification that I must do? It does not just happen at the beginning and then stop: it is continual, the first step in a finely choreographed dance between the interrogator and the prisoner. This dance is how I first establish and then strengthen the unique relationship I have with each prisoner. In fact, the dance is the relationship. I must control every nuance of the environment, to lead with sometimes a gentle hand, sometimes a firm one. Sometimes I don't even lead; I follow, using every sense to know where the killer will go. And then I ask a question, precisely, to lure a desired response. The art is in the improvisation: never knowing but always prepared, for I never know where the next step will lead. And I must remember that these men are ruthless, no matter how pitiful they may now seem, and so I must be equally ruthless in return.

Iraq, 2005

312 Days Remain

For the next three days I am on another Iraqi military base in Mosul. I am giving a class to all the Iraqi intelligence officers and soldiers who are in charge of prisoners. I'm teaching them on how to deal with detainees.

The job of transferring control to the Iraqi Security Forces is complex, and one part involves monitoring the welfare of detainees and getting people into and through the Iraqi legal system, along with seemingly countless other details.

After this first day of prisoner training, I head out to search a few of the houses near our base. Other than the mortar rounds that drop occasionally, we have been receiving sniper fire. So at around midnight I head out to search a building that I suspect the sniper uses as a perch. It is just another teammate and me, with about ten Iraqis. We knock and yell at the front gate; we demand, and still nothing, so tie a big rope around the metal bars and attach it to the front bumper of the HUMVEE. I yell "Go" and with a crash down comes the gate.

We push open the first door we come to.

Inside there are a few minutes of hysteria, but then we find that the house is the home of several prostitutes. It is a sad scene. In Iraq, prostitutes operate from home, and this house is the workplace of several women. The home is filled with dirty children and infants living in squalor. Mothers wrap arms around bundles of crying children, or else the children pile up in groups, hiding in the dark of room corners. One tiny little girl just stands there frozen and staring from the middle of the room, at these large men with guns, who yell and look under soiled mattresses. As her eyes glisten, her tears tear me apart.

Last night, we didn't find evidence of the tormenting sniper. Therefore, before today's prisoner training begins, I drive to the American base and meet with some Special Forces friends. I beg and plead, and eventually they let me borrow a sniper rifle—finally I can put my training to use. I'm planning to spend a few hours a day just sitting on my roof trying to find my friendly sniper's location, to deliver a well-deserved dose of retribution. It feels good to do something.

Every day brings something different; I do not get bored anymore. I tried calling Amy this morning but she was not home. It's been a rough few days, and I needed to hear her voice. I wanted to ask her how the documentary was that she saw, and to ask her about the workout she was excited about. Did I thank her for the thumb drive she sent me? I have so much going on, sometimes I forget if I just thought to myself to thank her or if I really did actually utter the words. It's hard to tell.

After the short drive to get the sniper rifle from my friends, I drive to the Iraqi base to begin the second day of prisoner training, which has been an interesting and rewarding experience. I'm using this tiny little classroom, ventilated only by small, rickety ceiling fans that wobble when they twirl.

The windows are covered with newspapers to keep the sun-light outside. The students are a mix of officers and enlisted, Kurds and Arabs, so the dynamics are rewarding to witness. The classes are on a wide array of subjects: human rights, the Geneva Convention, scene investigation, meal procedures, fire safety, and so on. I give a small class on something the Army calls the Five S's: Search, Segregate, Silence, Speed to the Rear, and Safeguard. The Army has a thousand and one mnemonic games and this one is about the process of handling a person who has just been caught.

As I stand in front of the small class, I look up at the twirling fan, and I swear the fan's in an uncontrollable wobble. So I take a step to the side, then I look down and read over my flash-cards. Sweat rolls down my face to pool in my chin dimple and sometimes the sweat splatters my notes, so I move my hands to the side so the drops won't smudge the pencil. Then I say one sentence in English, the Arab translator repeats it in Arabic, and then the Kurdish translator will listen to the Arabic translator and then re-translate it into Kurdish. It takes a long time to do a very short class, but it is fun; the classes are animated, with the students asking lots of questions, and during every class I find some way to talk about the humane treatment of prisoners. I am the American, after all.

During my class, we discuss Abu Ghraib and how to not allow this to happen here. "It is vital for the Iraqi citizen and the world community to respect and trust the Iraqi military." I speak about how it is the Iraqi officer's responsibility to monitor the prison guards and to avoid abusing prisoners. But it's frustrating, for both the Iraqi and I, since this last point of my lecture doesn't seem to resonate.

I always have to remember that I am dealing with a completely different culture. The Iraqi legal system is based on the confession. Confessions are what they look for, and confessions are all that is needed to find a person guilty, and so the confession is what the interrogator tries to get. As you might expect, this cultural trait drives interrogators to act in specific ways.

It seems so easy to say "No beating the prisoners," until I'm actually standing here teaching the same people who have been beaten themselves so often before. I wag my finger and explain "No beating the prisoners," but I can see their minds turning and them thinking "But this prisoner is a terrorist. He has killed women, children, or a soldier friend of mine. If he confesses he will go to jail, so I must get him to confess. Why should the world care if this requires that I hurt him? How typical of you hypocritical Americans."

It is a long road to change such deeply ingrained beliefs, and sometimes it feels like I am Sisyphus. I am conflicted about this as well. As an adviser, I am not in charge. I am not in control. I can only point in the right direction. But then there are times during the class when something clicks. "Not every person captured is guilty," I say. When I point this out, I think the Kurds and Shia, who've suffered so much under Saddam, and even some of the Sunnis, understand. When I explain that if you beat prisoners, you will be just as likely to have created a terrorist as to have stopped one, I get some nods and grunts of agreement.

I've been here for only a few months, but this short time seems like an eternity: countless patrols, playing chicken with fate, and then returning to my Iraqi base, where every night I confront the same people who want my death on the streets. They stumble dirty and blindfolded through the door, and every week I have to deal with some abuse that has taken place. My arguments against abuse aren't working, and I struggle with myself, wondering if I should even care.

I know abuse of prisoners was—and still is—used throughout the Middle East. Nowhere was this truer than in Iraq under Saddam Hussein. It is one of the reasons why torture is still used here, and one of the reasons why the Iraqis I work with are so successful at what they do. In Iraq, an interrogator will not turn away from this simple, if hard-to-swallow, fact: to gain a confession, torture almost always works. The potential of a false confession, in their minds, is worth the risk. Here, a confession is what's needed to put a terrorist, a killer, behind bars. So they use this knowledge to their advantage; if necessary, they make a person suffer in order to save an innocent. Cosmic justice, I would say, but most times such things are not necessary.

Most insurgents that we capture and interrogate are motivated more by personal benefit than by any religious or moral conviction. When we confront them with facts, they became weak and timid, most cry, and almost all soon just confess. They are afraid. They should be. Most terrorists dislike mental or physical discomfort; morbidly funny if you think about it. The terrorist's focus is on "How do I get myself out of this situation, or at least minimize the risk to myself?"

The Iraqis I work with use this knowledge to their advantage. Though torture is used, it seems that success comes more from the terrorist's own fear of torture than from any actual torture itself. The prisoner's imagination is often an interrogator's most powerful ally. But then there is the occasional anomaly where this maxim does not hold true: the devout Muslim terrorist, the man who believes that the more suffering he endures, the greater his pleasure in paradise will be.

But what is torture, anyway? It seems everyone has a different definition. Is it abacination, boiling, crushing, drilling, flaying, garroting, hamstringing . . . waterboarding? Is it putting a gun to a prisoner's head—"click"? Is it making the prisoner stand up and then sit down, over and over again? Is it giving him water but not letting him pee? What about sleep deprivation? Or detaining a relative? Is it releasing him and then letting the whole town know that he talked with me, the American? Is it telling him his nephew is sick and that he won't get to see him before the nephew dies? Is it having a fake doctor strip him to "check," then telling the town, his friends, family, and fellow terrorists that he is gay? No sunlight? No bed? No companionship? How about no window? Or refusing them a daily walk, outside? Is it not giving him chips, soda and a cigarette, before saying please? "Excuse me, sir, but could you kindly answer if you're a terrorist? Have you ever used a rusty and dull blade to saw off any heads?"

And then, I think on my own definition of what constitutes torture. Does my definition change depending on who I have in my prison cell? I know it does; I feel my bar adjust every single day. Yes, I am conflicted, but I have a responsibility to prevent what I consider meets my definition. No one has told me any different.

I am told "Teach, coach, mentor. Enable your counterpart." Why? "To capture and kill insurgents. Oh, and try to deter abuse in the process." How? "You're Special Forces. Use your experience and judgment." Well, that is what we get trained and paid for, and this is what I have done; so instead of crying that the sky is falling, I am going to work on changing the proclivities of my counterpart. I need to find an argument that's convincing.

So I've begun a more pragmatic approach. I appeal to strategic consequences.

"Look," I begin, "there are serious consequences if you torture prisoners. Just look at what happened in Abu Ghraib. The use of torture encourages international and—more importantly—local support for the terrorist's cause."

This line of reasoning doesn't seem to hold any water, so I try to appeal to tactical consequences. "Look, torture produces unreliable information. And if you torture a devout prisoner, this will just increase their resistance and will only prove to them that their cause is just. It's possible that you are torturing an innocent civilian who will eventually be released. These tales of abuse will spread in the community and only strengthen the citizens' support for the terrorist."

But this mostly gets me glazed and unbelieving looks.

I guess there is no black-and-white morality against torture, especially in Iraq. Is morality somehow different in war? Is wrong-and-right only black-and-white where choices are easy, where hard decisions are not necessary? Well, that is definitely not here in Mosul. When you move from the professor's abstract lecture to a dirty and dark basement prison filled with terrorists and surrounded by a city full of killers, the immediate benefit of torture is just more apparent.

Do my threats of "Just don't, or else" lack credibility? My lectures, my appeals, don't seem to hold sway. The Iraqis I work with just know that torture is justified in certain circumstances. Here they face the prisoner they believe is a terrorist, and who they have strong reason to believe has information about an innocent's imminent death. Here the use of mental and physical discomfort, or even pain, to induce talking is logical, and justified, and my attempt to deter abuse by an appeal to morality engenders only their contempt. And to argue based on law, or on utility? Fuck, no. This doesn't work either. I am just a soft, hypocritical American.

In Iraq, the present is reality, and taking action for an immediate and tangible benefit is far more preferable than not acting due to some uncertain benefit in their very uncertain future. So I have become desperate. I have begun to make use of the things Saedi values most: relationships, honor, his family, and his tribe. I use his friendship with me. I use these as levers to point out real-world consequences while simultaneously sympathizing with his perspective. It seems I am learning from Saedi. I'm manipulating.

I say: "I know that these terrorists are cowards who do not have human rights. I know they have information that may save some innocent. I, like you, have no sympathy for them. However, just listen to me. We are good friends and you know I will always be honest with you. If you torture them, you will get me into trouble. If you torture them, you risk the reputation of your unit. Your actions put me at risk: what if you torture an innocent person? These risks are just not worth the possibility that this asshole has information which he may tell us."

This particular pragmatic approach seems to work, at least for a while, but I know it is tenuously tied to our "friendship," to his respect for me. Together we capture terrorists, get them to confess, and so save innocents in the process. Then I use our friendship as a way to prevent his attempt to save innocents? Have I just become the very people I'm desperate to stop? By defending these people, have I raped a boy, or kidnapped a girl by proxy? Has my black-and-white coffeeshop reasoning killed an American? I see so no clear right or wrong choices, only shades between bad and worse. So I decide on my red line because not deciding is a choice—I decide on the chip that Saedi can't knock off: "Play mental games with these killers to your heart's content," I tell him. "But a kick, a slap, or more? No more." And I will just have to deal with the life-and-death consequences. I hope it's a compromise I can live with.

Germany, September 2011

20 Days Remain

I come awake and I stare into the dark of another morning. It's 4 A.M., and the swirl dreams still cloud my thinking. I sneak outside and sit on the tailgate of our SUV and listen to the dark for just a few seconds more.

Lately—since Landstuhl, I think—I'm starting to feel happy, inexplicably, not a care in the world. It's not right, though, this contrast, and it is disturbing. I have sudden new powers, special powers, powers that I can't explain. I am now more intelligent. So I spend my days thinking, and I no longer have any interest in eating. I don't feel hungry. And I don't sleep either, or at least, I sleep much less now. Not that I was sleeping much before, anyway. Sleep requires time that I can spend doing more important things, like thinking. I get up at all hours of the night, and then the earliest of the morning, to think and to write down my thoughts. I'm starting to look forward to the onrush of thoughts because I know that my insights are amazing, thought-provoking, and even world-changing. Some distant partition of me knows that this is delusional, but I feel it nonetheless, fervently so. I feel high on life, and my lack of food and sleep has no negative effect that I can tell. It feels like I can see and understand everything. Before, my thoughts were so slow. But now, I have such important thoughts that I have no interest in work at all; my thoughts are my only care.

Cheryl, who is aware of this change and worried, convinced me of our need to get away, so this weekend we are camping with the girls in Germany's Black Forest. So now here I sit, outside our tent in the dark and cold of 4 A.M.; and under the glow of my headlamp, I look down on my notes written on cardboard squares I cut from cardboard boxes I found in the trash can. I stare at what I've scribbled down. There are dozens of these squares filled with thousands of words that flow in various directions; some words and sentences are highlighted by underlines, arrows, smiley faces, exclamation points, question marks, and little desperately drawn stars. There is so much, I hope, that will help guide Cheryl to who I am but which I can't verbalize. My hope is that this scribbling will help bring me into focus; but right now, as I look down at this incessant scrawl, I see instead bloody fingernail scratches on the backside of a locked door. What do the marks mean?

Yes, I am flawed, but I know I can be better, for her and for the girls, and yes, I'm now different, but I still believe Cheryl and I are meant for each other.

Is this faith? Do I even have faith? Faith in what? Surely not the human race or myself: too much suffering for the absolution of those sins. But is it actually possible that some people are meant for each other? Or do I just need her, and this conviction just brings me happiness? And if I do find happiness, what does it matter if the belief is true or not? I know that the bliss I now feel is not real. It is surreal. But if happiness is what I feel, doesn't this make the emotion real?

It seems almost physically impossible to resolve this inner contradiction, the yawning chasm between my desire and my life experience. I feel high on life yet hopelessly brittle. Is this what it's like to be manic-depressive? But this can't be real. I'm not one of those people who get pointed at! I refuse to run to any professional. I refuse to drown under some pharmacological concoction or psychological drivel. I dug this hole, and I'll either lie down or climb out on my own.

Iraq, 2005

310 Days Remain

I stay in bed to write a letter to Amy, to tell her about some of the things that are happening, how last night some people were under attack, and how Iraqis came to the front gate looking for an American . . .

. . . I run to wake up an interpreter and go out to meet them; the night is warm and there is a breeze blowing and the tall trees are swaying and creaking. I hear the Iraqis talking while the wind is speaking. What I soon find out is that an Iraqi compound is under attack and they are asking for our help. This happens often—Iraqis coming to our gate asking for help. So I grab an interpreter's hand and we run to Saedi's office so they can point to a map and I can determine the location of this attack and get other clarifying details. I then run to our radio in our command post to call the American military. The interpreter is translating in my one ear while the Iraqis are on their cell phones talking loud and crying about friends dying. I relay this three-way, multi-lingual, cross-cultural dialogue, but the attempt to help is futile. Helping is hopeless here.

I try to describe all of this in my letter to Amy; but does she care? I just don't know anymore. So I pull off my blanket, roll out of bed, quietly lace my boots up, and sneak out the bedroom door.

It's 3 A.M. as I walk through our makeshift kitchen and grab a quick snack . . . a Cinnabon: so good, but so unhealthful. I push open our spring-loaded wood door and enter the early morning darkness of Mosul. It's quiet, but I still hear the rustling of a thousand birds nesting in the tall grass at river's edge. Night is when the wild dogs start to prowl and the feral cats come out from under the buildings. Night is also when Iraqi terrorists go to sleep. Lazy fucks. But not here at the Guest House. Here, the terrorists dread the dark; they fear the sound of distant footsteps becoming louder, and closer.

I shake these thoughts from my head and walk across the wet grass to enter Saedi's building—a building that, by the way, freaks me out with its sinister gloom and hidden rooms that I've never explored. I push these thoughts aside and descend the stairs to enter Saedi's room, to see him puffing on a cigarette and talking on two mobile phones at the same time.

He hangs up and we begin our ritual.

"Assalam u alaikum, Saedi. Sabah al Khair"; and what should take minutes will become hours. I despair. We sit and smoke and drink chai and he starts to tell me about the type of insurgent we interrogated last night, right before those Iraqis came to our front gate. He says we will do more interrogations later, but for the time being he wants to discuss the man we spent time with the night before.

"Mr. Bill. Let me tell you about this man, this Salafi Takfiri.

"Takfiris are persons of devout Islamic faith," he tells me. "But the difference is that these men will use every means at their disposal to kill unbelievers."

He explains how these men recruit disenchanted youths and the poor, the morally corrupt, and the criminal. How they have associations with Baathists and get assistance from the Intelligence Services of other countries. How they do not drive vehicles, do not use cell phones, and do not grow the traditional facial hair or wear the traditional clothing, which allows their fundamentalism to blend in. How they change locations weekly and use several names and how I should "consider these men as modern terrorists." "These are men," he continues, "who are not only just deeply religious and fanatically motivated, but who are often intelligent and willing to use any and all means to achieve their goal. If you want to be successful here, you must learn about these men, Mr. Bill."

He ends with a "Let's go look at this Takfiri," so we walk down to the cell and he has the guard untwist the metal tie and we look inside. He points with his eyes. "He is a strict Muslim with an exacting standard of how to lead a 'proper' life, Mr. Bill. This Takfiri is taught and conditioned to break every religious and moral code if they do so to advance their cause; God expects this and they will be forgiven," he tells me.

"The Wahabists of Saudi Arabia, the Islamic philosophers of Syria and Jordan, these are the thinkers of jihad, or holy war. The big objectives are theirs, and then these ideas are passed to the Takfiris here in Iraq, here in the city of Mosul. Within Mosul, most groups have at least one Takfiri within their ranks, and it is this person who is a cell's spiritual guide and who gives the group guidance and directives. The Takfiris then recruit from our community. Stopping this man should be our focus.

"When we spoke with this Takfiri last night, you were not talking with a normal murderer or killer for money. He believes he's an instrument of Allah's will. He's driven by absolute certainty. This is a man who considers us non-believers, and they think the Iraqi people are unbelievers for supporting you and for wanting democracy. If we pressure him in the cell, if we abuse him, he believes God will help and will come to his aid; and if he dies, then he will be guaranteed admittance to Paradise."

Saedi whispers: "When we come back in to interrogate this man, what we must do is agree to his attacks against Americans and say that this is good. Say that God is on his side and thankfully he did not attack Iraqis. Identify with his beliefs, and sometimes this leads to a confession of killing Americans—usually not, but as he talks about his attacks, he forgets, and then he will make mistakes. One mistake is that you cannot attack Americans without sometimes also attacking Iraqi police or the Iraqi Army. If you attack Americans, civilians are often in the way and they get killed as well. This is when I get him!" he accentuates with a fist striking an open palm.

"But know that this Takfiri is very careful; that even with physical and mental pressure, he will be the most resistant to providing you information. His faith in Allah and his belief in the rightness of his cause are absolute. To this man, any interrogator of a Takfiri is an unbeliever. It is his belief that when he is captured and confronted, that this only reaffirms his belief in his cause, and it is confirmation that Allah is with him. Fear of pain, fear of his fellow terrorists, any hopes for economic gain or loss of respect, any possibility of leniency, and the loss of his life, all of these things will not work. So getting this man to talk will take weeks or even months, and here in Iraq we do not have such a long time to focus on this man. We must get information quickly to save a life tonight or maybe in the morning. Therefore, you must quickly identify which prisoner is a Takfiri so that you can focus your efforts instead on the weaker people that usually surround him. Use them, these weak ones, use the information that they give you so you can then keep this Takfiri in jail."

It's now approaching sunrise and our impending interrogation of this Takfiri, and our need to find the weak link in his group.

I am tired, and I really want to go to bed, but I ask another question instead. I can't seem to help myself.

"How can I quickly identify these men, these Takfiris?"

"There is a small but very important Sura, which they know and often use, and the recitation of this Sura is like reading 33 percent of the Koran. The Takfiris are trained on this verse and of its importance. A terrorist who is being interrogated is under a huge amount of stress, and so they seek the emotional support that comes from this prayer. So when we ask if they are religious and then we tell them to prove their devotion by reciting their favorite verse, the Takfiri will often cite this one Sura. And when pressed, they will answer with 'Allah Musa'ed,' which means 'God who is helping.' I will teach you this Sura, Mr. Bill.

"But remember," he continues, after another quick puff on his cigarette, "this Salafi Takfiri is different from a Muslim who is a terrorist, because he's devout. These men are just religious and are doing attacks only because they think that their actions are right and you are morally wrong. These are believers who do not believe all non-believers must die. With these men, these religious men, the interrogator must discuss religion. So you must get to know Islam. We tell them that even Mohammed the Messenger— 'alayhi as-salām—allied himself with the Jews and Christians when he was in trouble and when he escaped. This person believes he is moral and you are a moral man acting immorally. With these, discuss only wrong and right. But no matter what, remember this one most important thing: do not deny a Muslim his prayers nor denigrate Islam, and do not show him you are not religious or that you do not believe in the one God. If you do this, all will be lost.

"Ask instead if he has been given time to pray, and show anger if he has not. With these men, only discuss the Koran and the teachings of Mohammed—'alayhi as-salām. Show them respect. This will create rapport, and in some cases this will be enough to get a religious man who does terrorism because he is moral to see that he is wrong: that you are also a moral man whom he misunderstands. Someday, we will capture one of these men and then I will ask you for your assistance. I will ask for you to just talk with him so that he can see that his assumptions are wrong."

Germany, September 2011

19 Days Remain

We left the campground, and we were going to drive straight home but it was already getting late. We were tired, the kids were screaming, so we found a hotel instead.

It is now morning, and Cheryl and the kids are still sleeping . . . and I'm pulled awake with another sinking feeling.

I sneak out of the hotel room to wind down the stairs . . . *and I step off the bottom step, feel a transition, then land on the basement floor to smell the mildew that stains the walls. I start walking down the hallway, and then I see a dim light. It's coming from a distant room far down to the right. I move forward, slowly, and then I turn right to enter the hotel reception area. . . .*

I want some coffee, but no one is around. It's 5 A.M. Shouldn't someone be here? I ring the bell. I want to ask when breakfast is served, but no one is here, or hears. I ring again, and there is a sign in German on the counter. Aha! "No receptionist until 7 A.M. and breakfast served at 7:30." I wait. Finally, I see a waitress. My hands are waving. I love trying to speak German even though I'm horrible. I am able to tell her that my kids are sleeping, I am tired but I can't sleep so I now really, really need the coffee that isn't served until 7:30 A.M. I smile. Thank you! I love my early morning coffee. I bounce outside to sit on the porch. The sun is rising, the weather is cold, and I'm desperately happy.

I peruse my cardboard squares. I add a squiggle. Or two.

8:45 A.M.
My daughters are with me and we gaze out on this beautiful valley of grapevines. I smile and then I sit down. I pull Ava off my leg and tell the angels to go corral their mommy. I return to my squares and I smile but inside, behind the mask, I am scared because I am thinking, and thinking, and thinking.

9:02 A.M.
What prevents me from understanding what is happening to me? Is this a lack of connections in my brain between emotion and reason? I need these connections. It's painful without them. And terrifying. Can I somehow regrow these connections? I think, therefore I am, right?

9:03 A.M.
My never-ending thinking led to an understanding.
There actually is a GOD.
Did He hear?!
He did.
I'm born again and crying. . . .

**358 Days Remain: Preparing the vehicles to travel from Baghdad
to my new home of Mosul**

I came to Iraq 4 years after 9/11 and was eager to meet some equally fanatic Islamists,
and to then kill them. I would also live with Iraqis. I would work, eat, and fight with
them. I was looking forward to this: I hungered for the field that would test my mettle.
Finally, I had arrived.

353 Days Remain: Suicide vehicle bomb during Mosul area-familiarization patrol

For the next year, this was my home: a stew of religions, ethnicities, and tribes all seeking revenge for some wrong. Mosul was a city so consumed by the past that it no longer had a present. Mosul was chaos.

**349 Days Remain: The Guest House as seen from my rooftop
(prison located below, and to left of the pickup truck)**

I lived on the banks of the Tigris River in the center of Mosul. It was a run-down home, with waterless fountains, overgrown rose bushes, and empty pools filled with razor wire. There was a beauty to the dystopia. But if you scratched, darkness would rise to the surface.

342 Days Remain: Saedi interrogating two brothers

Beneath an unremarkable 3-story building, I studied a fine art from a practicing master:
how to look into the mind and heart of a killer, and then be able to say "I know you as
well as myself." I had to become this.

324 Days Remain: Iraqi soldiers in formation inside the Guest House
Iraq was so different, so unfamiliar. But I understood the need for the stomping feet
and swinging arms of the formation; every day, Iraqis and Americans were dying. Do
what's necessary. Do what works.

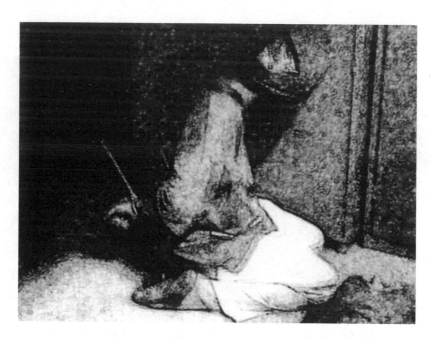

323 Days Remain: Waiting for his interrogation

I studied the forms that Saedi performed: he was nice, mean, angry, and then happy. He'd hit, slap, hurt, and scare. Then he would sympathize, and then exude sorrow before going deathly quiet. Then he would move close to whisper an intimate story. But I wasn't able to wear these masks. I felt only hate toward the killer of women and children.

**320 Days Remain: Sunset over the Tigris River
with old-town Mosul in the distance**
When I needed to breathe, I would stand on the banks of the Tigris. There was a calm
in a sunset seen through razor wire, and thoughts of Amy grilling salmon.

318 Days Remain: The tactical interrogation

Soon, one lesson stood out from the rest: bad people do bad things because they can, and good people making hard decisions can stop them. But I was conflicted. It was my responsibility to protect the captured terrorists from the people he terrorized. I also had to consider the "terrorist," the possibly innocent. So I had to decide on a red line I was not willing to cross, and then just live with the life and death consequences.

312 Days Remain: Returning from a midnight raid

Life was a never-ending cycle—collecting intelligence, capturing insurgents, and then interrogating the insurgents that we captured so we could capture more. During one operation, we didn't find the sniper we were looking for, but we did make a little girl cry. Is wrong-and-right only black-and-white where choices are easy, where hard decisions are not necessary? Is morality different in war?

**310 Days Remain: Takfiri leader and his assassination cell
(signs read "The Terrorist")**

One week, we captured an entire terrorist cell, to include their hateful leader. Then we
spent the next week pitting one against the other. In the end, we put their pictures in
the local paper and said they were terrorists who confessed. But it was futile; in a few
weeks they'd be back on the streets to kill again. No matter what we did, we didn't make
a difference. We just dug holes in dry sand.

Iraq, 2005

309 Days Remain

Saedi agrees to go out for a walk with me; it was just too damn smoky and smelly in his basement office. Saedi, three Iraqi soldiers, two interpreters, and three informants chain-smoking in a fifteen-by-twenty-foot space was just too much.

It's almost midnight and the moon is out. We walk slowly around the half-mile of road that skirts the bank of the Tigris. My arms are behind my back and there is a dip in my mouth. I look up at the sky, I search for distant stars to change my focus, but it doesn't work: my mind returns to our prison and how in a ten-foot square, simple human interactions lead to surprising emergent phenomena. How does that happen?

And so I ask Saedi, "How do you know what to do or say in an interrogation?"

The wild dogs yip and bark, a distant gunshot echoes, and Saedi replies: "When I start interrogating a person or group, I start with the belief that they are guilty, and my interrogation either supports my belief or begins to prove me wrong."

"But how do you know if someone is guilty?"

"I pepper them with questions. I ask when, where, why, how, and demand quick answers. Because I know the details, I compare his answers. If his answer is ready and quick, my first instinct is that he may be innocent. It is the guilty man who thinks."

We have been walking now for ten minutes, and any more would be considered exercise to him. So we head back to his office.

We arrive, socialize for a while, and then we go to sit in a small cinderblock cell. There is a small table between us, and today's prisoner sits on the floor sniveling and shivering. I stand in the rear, wearing a black mask. There is another man, also in a mask. He is an Iraqi jundee who is here to only take notes. I pretend I am just taking notes as well. We can't very well let the prisoner know there is an American in this Iraqi interrogation. He wouldn't talk if he knew. When it comes to the Americans, the insurgents seem to have nothing to fear. This rule applies to the prisons but not to the streets—a really strange thing, now that I think about it.

In the American military prison, the American interrogators have been effectively castrated: they abide by every rule to protect each killer. But on the streets the American military minimize, circumvent, and sometimes even forget every possible rule, disregard every consequence, make every conceivable effort just so we can kill him. Saedi tells me that he thinks insurgents even want to get caught by Americans. Theirs is a tough life, and Saedi and I share a sentiment about the terrorist's perspective: "at least in American prisons I can get some rest and recharge in order to kill again."

I realize Saedi is still talking to the prisoner, so I start to pay attention. Saedi walks toward the rear of the cell where I stand. He leans in close to whisper so the man on the floor cannot hear broken English, but then he quickly switches to complicated Arabic, so the interpreter quietly translates in my ear: "This man is called Saud. He once worked with Abu Sana, who was a big terrorist. At the beginning of his first interrogation, he did not speak. He says 'I did work with Abu Sana one time, but have stopped terrorism.' His answers are very slow."

"Slow, slow, slow, were his answers," Saedi later tells me in his office. "We did not let him sleep. We made him walk outside in the cold and did not let him use the restroom. And then by chance we saw on the news that Abu Tahan, a very big terrorist, had been detained. So in the cell I told the terrorist this, and he asked 'Abu Tahan was detained?'

"This was a blow to his morale, and he looked scared, and it made me think 'Why would this have an impact on Saud?' So I tell him I know. 'You worked with Abu Tahan, and did you know he is in the cell next door? No? It is interesting, the things he says.'

"After this, Saud gave us the whole details of his cell. Saud broke because we told him that right now you are in the Iraqi Directory of Intelligence and we know everything about you. Every lie will be known; if you want to be released quickly, then confess, and in six months you will be back out. But if you don't talk, you will stay here and we have no other duties but to focus on you.' And so he gave up."

"But he is afraid." I ask. "What if he confesses to things he did not do so he can be let out in only six months?"

"It sometimes happens, but we often will find out. You remember the entire IED emplacement cell we captured? Before those eight men were dropped off here at the Guest House, we did not have any informants on this group. So sometimes we must use family for information so we can say 'We know you were in this house' or 'You drove your friends' car at this time,' and these statements make them afraid. We didn't have anything on this group and these were all difficulties. But I believed that one man was innocent; I told my assistant to question him anyway to find out his personal details.

"This man then claimed to have made a car bomb, and he went on to provide details about where he made it. We asked him, 'How did you make the explosive?' He said 'We put grenades in the car.' Grenades in a car for a car bomb? Come on. We know this doesn't work. He claimed to have attacked the Iraqi police and he said they fought them for one hour. He lied about these things, he confessed to things we know he did not do, because we made this man miserable. This was all that was needed to break him, and so he confessed to things he never did. We asked him: 'Why did you lie?' He said, 'Sir, you destroyed me! That slap was so strong that I thought if this was your slap, what happens if you use a cable!'"

~

I wake up early to prepare for our day's patrol.

Today, I am the turret gunner, which means I am up on top of our vehicle, exposed, while everyone else is down below, enclosed behind armor and two inches of bulletproof glass, which for some of us is counterintuitively not reassuring: HUMVEE armor sucks.

The traffic is horrendous as we cross a big bridge that links the city east to west. As we cross, I find myself surrounded by cars, stuck in standstill traffic and unable to move no matter how much I honk or yell. This is something you do not want to happen, and it is terrifying. I am the gunner in the lead vehicle, so I concentrate on what's in front and to the immediate left and right of us. My job as the gunner is to always remain alert, and to be especially vigilant when coming into intersections, when on freeways, and passing on-ramps and overpasses. The gunner's primary responsibility is to ensure that traffic does not come upon us suddenly and that other cars do not get too near. And if they do, I must get them to stop. If they refuse, then I must shoot.

This can be a very difficult situation, because in a split second you must decide whether a car that does not stop is a suicide bomber or if it is just an inattentive driver; and you have to make this decision early enough so that if the car is a threat, there is still enough time to stop it before it gets too close. It is incredibly stressful up there on top of the vehicle in the midst of a sprawling metropolis, knowing that in the midst of hundreds of thousands of innocents are a few insurgents in roaming cars looking to blow you up.

Today, after the mission, I try to think of a way to explain this to Amy. I usually stay quiet about my reality, but today I decide to break my silence.

"Imagine," I say, "that you are in downtown D.C. and that you know, I mean really *know*, that somewhere there is a car, or several cars, loaded with explosives and that the person in each of these vehicles wants you dead. Now imagine that these drivers know exactly what make and color of car you drive. Also imagine that somewhere, along the roads that you use, are one or many more roadside bombs, just waiting for you to pass by. And then imagine that you have no choice but to drive for hours, to daily just wander around, and around, and around. I mean, fuck, each patrol is a driving version of Russian Roulette."

So, I tell Amy, you must protect your team, and yourself, by choosing or not choosing to shoot. And you sure do not want to shoot someone who does not mean you harm. But you also do not want to take a chance; you do not want to hesitate, for more than just your own life is at stake. So you just have to decide, in a split second, whether or not to shoot. Is it just an innocent car that just happens to have no passengers? Is it a terrorist? Maybe. But you must decide quickly. Decide! Is it a car just going fast, heading in your direction, or is it a terrorist careering forward, belted into a bomb with wheels? Decide! No time to contemplate! And how about that car with the shocks loaded down as if carrying lots of weight? Terrorist? Maybe. Decide, now! Lives hang in the balance! How about that car coming into the intersection from our right, the car that does not stop when you wave your non-firing hand? Who does not stop when you point your weapon? Who does not stop even when you finally take a warning shot into the street? Terrorist? Maybe. Decide—now!—because you have a micro-second remaining before you must shoot him in the chest. Decide! Terrorist? Or just some stupid-ass whose kids are screaming and whose wife is nagging about how he never buys her presents? Or that car that does not yield as the driver merges onto the freeway from your right? Terrorist? Maybe. The clock is ticking! No time is left! Most likely he is just someone who is listening to the radio, who doesn't see you. And the farmer on the sidewalk carrying sticks on a donkey? You're stuck in traffic, you see him slowly come toward you from your rear. Terrorist? Is that Death being pulled close by a rope? Is there a bomb hidden within that bushel? Should I point and yell "Stop"? Should I shoot? Or should I crash into the car to our front—the one with the kids peeking out the rear window—their eyes are wide, should I crash into them, push them out of the way so I can move away? Or do I shoot the donkey guy? Or should I just let the donkey and handler pass, move on by, and smile and accept whatever happens?

I mean really, there are thousands of these scenarios each and every day, and each one comes down to this: the choice of life, or death.

Do I save myself and risk killing an innocent? What about the Americans I'm with? It's all about how we weigh choices: how much risk am I willing to accept before I kill a possibly innocent person? And consciously or not, every American fighting an insurgency feels some version of this—the ever-present press of a barrel to the temple, and then the "Click," over and over again, hundreds, thousands, tens of thousands of times, over and over again, and knowing that sooner or later the universe will demand remittance. It's pure statistics.

But if you focus on each and every choice, the countless chances of death, it will drive a person insane.

I go back on a patrol tonight, and out again tomorrow, and then the day after next, and then there are 300-plus days more. I've come to realize that you cannot ever focus on the possibility, the reality of dying. Doing so will only lead to a paralyzing fear, which will then just make life even more dangerous. It is a fascinating conundrum that danger leads to fear, and that uncontrolled fear increases your danger. So instead, you must focus on the moment and not dwell on potentials. Use your left hand to wave at the kids who peer through the car's rear window, while your right index finger lies comfortably next to the trigger. Smile at the man on the cell phone while simultaneously staying alert, ready to shoot him in the chest at the slightest intuition. But after a while of living in a constant state of fear, I've started to adjust, to just accept that if I die it is fate and it was just meant to be.

And, amazingly, this complete submission is not terrifying. Instead, I now live in a place that is in the middle, a place between hyper-alert and unconscious, and this place is, well, enjoyable; it's extremely peaceful, and I find I smile as I drive. In fact, after a patrol, when I come home alive, I have the most dreamless sleeps that I have ever had. Even more interesting, I am starting to want to be the gunner, on the roof of my vehicle, with my head exposed. Knowing that death is so close makes me feel intensely, and intensely living is absolutely addictive.

Germany, 2011

19 Days Remain

I open an eye to see grains of wood, and then I look up to see the sun rising. I feel the trigger touching my finger, so I look down to see I'm holding a pencil that's on my notepad . . . there are squiggly lines everywhere on the page . . . and I realize it's morning and this is a porch in Germany . . . I'm crying, because God found me. And then the craziness continues relentlessly.

> 9:15 A.M.
> *I love my family (God really knew this was true!)*
> *There was conflict that I felt would lead to hurting my family*
> *I "wanted" to fix intensely*
> *I "needed" to fix immensely*
> *I "somehow" was able to truly "understand" nature of existence. What God intends*
> *Infused with "holy spirit" to allow true understanding?*
> *Determined how humanity could live in peace*
> *God's intention is Utopia!*
> *Understanding God's intention allowed me to understand God's intention?*

9:18 A.M.

I am a good person. I married a better person. Had two beautiful children. Experienced true love. Sensed loss of true love possible. So wanted to fix, to correct myself. I wanted and therefore the impossible became possible.
God exists
I didn't believe
But Cheryl did!
I felt TRUE LOVE?

9:20 A.M.

Question: Is there a God?
Answer: Yes?
Why: Because "I think therefore I am" became possible?
I made a misjudgment
God Exists and I don't know why I know.
Is this faith?
I feel certainty, but somehow there is wrongness eating me.
God, help me. God, leave me.

Iraq, 2005

290 Days Remain

It's evening, and before another round of interrogations I decide to sit down on my rooftop to think and write about the Americans who I see on TV, the ones who disagree with this war, with me, and with what I am doing.

"It does not feel like a war," I tell my parents in the letter I'm writing.

The word "war" has somehow evolved to mean "wrong" for most people. Since I do not feel that fighting is inherently wrong, "struggle" is the word I choose to describe this life. But then, my viewpoint may be a little too focused. Still, it is my right to have this opinion: this is my fucking experience, and being fed a stream of news from around the world in short sound bites can also make one who knows a little about everything know nothing about one thing.

Earlier this evening I was hanging out in the room where our interpreters live. Every one of them has an amazing story. This evening they were watching the al-Iraqiya news channel, and I try to absorb their wisdom. The mosque bombings had just occurred, and callers were phoning in to speak about their feelings, about the terrorists who had been caught. My friends narrated these calls, reactions that ranged from anger at the terrorists to anger at the government. The last caller was extremely angry at the government. He felt that the government was just too lenient with terrorists, and that this soft treatment of terrorists led to the atrocity of the bombing; he wanted the government to immediately execute these four men.

I ask the group of interpreters, "The terrorists kill civilians more than anyone else. Why does the populace accept their presence?" "They don't accept them," one interpreter responds. "But what we are seeing are the successful terrorist attacks. People are calling in tips, whole villages start up neighborhood watches."

It's good to hear this from someone who calls Iraq home, to hear that some people care and don't look away. Because in most places, it is easy to avoid the dark side of humanity, to personally not see the faces and hear the voices of those who enjoy hurting. But not here on this base. Here, I cannot look away: it's impossible for me to not wade through the very worst of my race.

I watched a Western movie last night, and in the final scene, the killer begs for mercy. "Why is it," the lawman asks, "that those who beg for mercy are the very same who never give it?" Living here gives this fiction life. And life isn't fiction. Not here.

Daily I read the secret reports and hear the words of the bomb-makers, the suicide bombers, and the financiers and counterfeiters who make the money so they can then pay for more foreign fighters, suicide bombers, IEDs, kidnappers, assassination squads, secret meetings, weapon caches, chemical weapons, and just about any other possible variation of terror that an imaginative mind can conjure up. And at the very same time, information about these terrorists comes streaming over cell phones from Iraqi civilians to Saedi and me. People are sick and tired of such acts, at least I like to think so.

Last night I sat with Saedi in his office as he juggled three cell phones and scribbled on a small white ruled notepad. The electricity was out and our only illumination was from a flashlight standing upright so the beam reflected off the ceiling. We discussed the information he just received; we looked at maps. I give advice. He thinks. He makes more phone calls, and more phone calls are answered. This scene is played out night after night, and sometimes, when things work out just right, I see the result in the cramped prison cell where devils beg for mercy.

Three nights ago I sat in a small room with hard walls, low lights, and the smell of mildew, and I watched and listened from two feet away as a young man described the evil that he did.

Restraint is difficult: I am starting to want to hurt them.

But I remind myself that this is only one version of the world, and that in *this* world I must protect the killer from his victim. It's lonely, and both obscene and absurd. It is becoming harder and harder to maintain perspective and to stay in control of myself.

Here at the Guest House, I give advice on the rule of law in a lawless society. I try to instill morality in a place devoid of human decency. I struggle with this role as I sit in these small cells and feel these evil men consume me. I want to hurt them, and that makes me afraid. I understand that there is a possibility that some of them are actually innocent: there is always this possibility in any prison, in any society. But here it is different. In a counterinsurgency the innocent always become entangled in the net made for sharks; so as I listen to these men proclaim their innocence, the possibility that they might actually be innocent makes me wince. I don't want this power over life: it is real and forever. I'm conflicted; but still I have a duty, and my weakness doesn't absolve me of a horrible responsibility.

Saedi may be in charge of this prison, but I am here to give advice, to teach, and to temper. The knowledge that I can suddenly appear at any time to see his prisoners and inspect his cells is probably the only reason that more abuse does not occur. But there are often successes, small steps that offset my decreasing sense of accomplishment. The prisoners are fed, washed, their cells cleaned, they are given water to drink, and they're kept out of the scorching sun. They are treated humanely—well, sort of—because here what is "humane" is relative. And if the guards do not really understand why, they do acknowledge the rules that I have set for them.

A few days ago, I took a short trip to transport five terrorists to another Iraqi prison. It was about 105 degrees in the glaring sun, and the prisoners were downloaded from the back of a Nissan pickup truck. One prisoner goes slower than the guards would have preferred, and a young Iraqi Army officer was a little more forceful than he should have been. He began to hit and kick the prisoner. I grabbed his arm and said "No."

I sometimes forget that public admonitions in this culture are much more emotionally traumatizing than in the American military. Later this young officer, deeply shamed, spoke to me through an interpreter. "Last week my friend was kidnapped," he explains. "That man is the one who killed him. I am sorry." He tells me that he understands why he should not do this. I'm proud that my admonition worked, but also sore, for a part of me doesn't feel my "no" *should* work.

Back home, these dilemmas are philosophical—over a double mocha latte, these choices seem so fucking simple. Don't abuse a prisoner. Turn the other cheek. Be the better person. But here? Here, the Iraqi guard is sorry for this action, but this doesn't mean he won't think it is necessary to be sorry again. When he does, I will grab his arm again and say "No." But the longer I live here, the less I want to make these corrections, the less I want to say "Never. On no account." They have a reason for each and every hurt, and it's getting difficult to reject their reasoning. Sometimes I too want to hit, kick, and slap these killers. Sometimes I want to do more.

Germany, September 2011

19 Days Remain

I raise my arms to stretch and reach back to break the surface; I open my eyes tight to the memories that now come so clearly and so increasingly, so unexpectedly. In a flash, I find myself looking at a man on the cold cement floor whimpering, and I feel the under-the-skin-crawling sensations that move me to whisper dark secrets to deserving ears . . .

. . . and the sliding glass doors open behind me. The early morning sun hits me . . . I'm still on the porch of the hotel, and thinking and thinking. . . .

"Your daughter Natalie sure is friendly. How old is she?"

I look up to see an elderly German man who introduces himself. His name is Ernst. His question surprises me, but I am eager for some German language practice. I desperately need a break from myself, so Ernst and I sit and pass pleasantries and personal histories as we juggle two languages and vast age differences.

"I retired five years ago," he tells me, running his hands through thinning gray hair. "My job was to take care of the British and American soldiers who were stationed in Germany."

"British soldiers?" I ask, not knowing the Brits were still stationed in Germany.

"Yes," he says. "I have been taking care of them since 1949. I was eleven when the German government gave me this job."

He talks about being a boy, taking care of Allied soldiers, and doing this for three quarters of a century. And I talk about being an American soldier and about this new state of forever war. We quickly find common ground. He smiles, and perceptions suddenly change. Ernst and I are very much the same.

Iraq, 2005

286 Days Remain

"Would you consider Abud a worker?" I ask Saedi as we wander back from the cell where we'd spoken with this man.

"Yes," he replies. "Abud is an example of the largest number of insurgents. He is a worker, which means he is the insurgent who kills for selfish reasons and not for religious or for moral or political reasons." He tells me that here in Iraq, workers come from every class and can be any age. The four men we detained last night are a perfect example. They all look different—some young, some old, some intelligent, some very stupid—but when we interrogate, I've learned to never make the mistake of thinking I know who the terrorist is, because a killer can be anyone. To think otherwise is just too simple and superficial; here everyone wears a mask to hide what's inside.

I've come to realize that it's impossible to disentangle the terrorist from the common criminal and that the dynamics of this conflict are much the same as any violent urban inner city. The primary difference is our labels. For example, "insurgent" and "terrorist," are both labels used to describe a person's intent and to create and sustain a specific mindset in the counterinsurgent: me. Labels allow us to deny another's humanness, and the more belittling the branding, the easier it is to "do what is necessary." This is particularly true for the terrorist: to them, I'm the "American," the "American Soldier," the "Occupier," and then the "Kafir."

Our walk has ended, so I follow Saedi into his office. I sit down in my regular old chair to stir and then drink my cup of chai. My mind wanders when I am here; it is so damn hard to focus anymore. There is the language difference; one of us speaks, it is translated, the other responds, and most of the time I have to repeat my words because the response I get back makes no fucking sense. Then I think "It must be the interpreter's bad translation," so I try again. Sometimes the translations are correct; it's just that the response is on a different wavelength—at least it doesn't make sense to me. So I try to work out what he may really be trying to say.

There are repetitions of things already said and the constant small talk about things that have nothing to do with anything at all. Cell phones ring—everyone's cell phone, all the time—so, of course, I must politely wait to continue talking, or wait for someone else to continue listening. Soldiers come and go, bringing updates, questions, and the constant refills of this god-awful-I-am-going-to-pull-out-my-own-back-hair overly sweet chai.

Then there are Saedi's tangents. First, we talk about the terrorist in our cell who has just confessed to raping and then killing some man's sweet daughter. Then, without warning, bam! Now he's yelling at me for not allowing him to torture his prisoners. "You don't let me be tough on terrorists! How can I do my job?" And then he starts working his prayer beads.

As the conversation heats up, Saedi's eyes start to bulge; his veins pop and his fingers pull and pull the prayer beads in a constant loop, moving faster and faster. "Just stop!" I want to yell. Damn, it's distracting. Then there is the thick soup of cigarette smoke that burns my eyes, which gives me constant headaches, and the "schhhhh . . . schhhhh" in the back corner as a soldier sprays tobacco-scented air-freshener. Tobacco; they just can't get enough of the stuff. And, oh my God, the TV! The TV is always on. The TV in this room runs a constant loop of Iraqi soap operas, which always cast a funny little Iraqi dwarf pulling some silly antic. In Iraq, the dwarf fills the role of the court jester and lord, are these jesters stupid. But now, God help me, they've decided to instead stream in the Kurdish version of MTV, which becomes a pervasive and cloying white noise.

These Kurdish versions of music videos always have some twist on the same old and tired theme. There is a young, good-looking Kurdish couple in traditional dress. They walk in a mountain meadow, through knee-high, bending grass. Their palms reach out to brush over the waving tops as they croon about eternal love, weaving in a story line of Kurdish ethnic superiority, freedom-fighting prowess, a poor mother who waits for the return of her Peshmerga son, or the plight of a beautiful culture under the hand of oppression.

My mind wanders, so I return to the office and I think that Saedi was talking; but now I see Iraqi jundees enter the room, and I preempt their attempt to refill my glass with a "la, shukran" as two cell phones ring. Saedi picks one up and hands the other phone to his assistant. So I wait . . . some more. I look over at the TV and, of course, there is a Kurdish woman handing a Peshmerga fighter a bundle of food while some odious pop melody plays in the background.

"Afwan, Saedi" I apologize, not realizing he is now off the phone and talking to me.

"Mr. Bill," he repeats, "I was saying that terrorist leaders recruit workers by knowing what they want, mostly by knowing their greedy needs. But now terrorist leaders can recruit by invoking the occupation. This inspires many."

He goes on to say that this is especially true among young Iraqis who are bored and lack motivation, Iraqis who are angry or want direction. Terrorist leaders provide them with the excitement and adventure they're seeking. The terrorist leader seeks to recruit the young man with a rich family or the man who wants quick-and-easy spending money. They seek out businessmen from whom to extort money. They call these men on the phone or show up at their business and say "You will provide us fifty dollars every week," or "We will use your business to have meetings." The terrorists will force some men to purchase weapons or hide explosives. They tell them "You must do these things or we will kill you." A more powerful tactic is when an honest person is told "If you don't do what we ask, we will take your wife or your daughter." The terrorist looks for the unintelligent man and says "I see that you suffer. Here is twenty dollars." Later, this twenty dollars becomes a cell phone and with it the request "When you stand here, can you call me if you see an American patrol?"

"We do not hate the Iraqi police or Americans," terrorist leaders will say to these workers who they put on a rooftop or street corner with a cell phone. "It is just that sometimes people get hurt by accident when the Americans shoot, so we want to be able to warn people when they come so Iraqis can stay inside." Or it is the herder who is asked to carry explosives or weapons on his donkey for a few dollars. This gets evidence out of the vehicle and onto animals that the Americans seldom notice. Or the Takfiri leader looks for the "lost" but religious youth who seeks discipline and guidance. The Takfiris are now disguising themselves as pious religious men who are fighting "unjust occupation by the horrible Americans."

Many workers are manipulated into the insurgency through these means, Saedi tells me.

"So yes, Abud is a worker," he says, "and they are becoming easier to recruit, because leaders now say that their reason is to liberate Iraq from Americans. To succeed, the terrorists must show that our government cannot provide security. They do this by conducting attacks and killing civilians. This, they say, is the only path to change.

"But know this, Mr. Bill," Saedi continues. "Only three things are needed for this to be successful: a terrorist leader who recruits, organizes, motivates, and guides; workers willing to carry out the leader's guidance; and, most importantly, Iraqi civilians who are willing to look away."

"But these people who kill for personal gain existed long before the Iraq War," I tell him. "They will always be a part of a society."

"Yes. But what is important," Saedi says, "is that because you are here and how poorly Americans treat Iraqis, the worker is now easier to recruit and the citizen is more willing to just look away. You now give them their motivation, and it will only get worse."

⌐

I reinforce my "Ma'a Salama, Saedi" with a wave good-bye. I walk out the door of his office to head back to the American command post, what we call the TOC, Tactical Operations Center.

For the last fifteen minutes, I had taken a break from my duty in the TOC in order to check on the health of the prisoners, which is necessary, but I'm starting to not want to do this. It's hard to care about horrible people, to ensure that they're healthy and taken care of; but I tell myself that the checkups are not about caring for the killer, it's about saving the life of an innocent—it's the information the prisoner may have—and also, if these men get sick and die, where's the justice in that?

I change my chain of thought as I arrive back at our TOC, the small room that we use for our maps, radios, and computers. Every night, one of us is required to stay up and be in the TOC, and tonight is my turn. While I listen to the radio, I study some Arabic. Or write an e-mail. Tonight's letter was a short one to Amy.

I go over the details of my trip home for Christmas. I sense she's resisting my plan for us to go to California; I tell her it's okay but point out that if I don't go, I will have missed two Christmases with my family. Also, it is Amy's birthday, so I tell her to go to the Lebanese Taverna to open her present and have a glass of red wine—just like we always did—and to imagine me sitting next to her. I tell her how much I love her, but something seems wrong between us. Maybe it's this place, which makes "us" seem so distant. But I have a whole night in this TOC so I finish my e-mail and start thinking about something else. I decide to write my parents and to describe my daily rituals.

On normal days I study Arabic at least twice, from 8 to 9 A.M. and 7 to 8 P.M. My evening lessons sometimes include our Iraqi interpreters. Today, for instance, I sat down with Ivan (Sunni Kurd), Hashim (Shia Persian), Ali (Yazeydi Kurd) and Maher (Sunni Arab). We sat in their room drinking the ever-present chai. I learn so much more than the Arabic language in these sessions, where we discuss everything from religion to politics and culture. Hashim, an older gentleman with a gray beard, was an English teacher during the Saddam era and is also a religious and moral philosopher. He is a learned and peaceful man who absolutely despises the terrorists and will speak for hours on how they have subverted the words of Allah and the teachings of Mohammed to justify their killing.

I take a break from my pondering and walk outside to speak with Amy on the cell phone. She had opened the birthday present I sent but didn't take my advice from the e-mail a few hours ago—she didn't go to the Lebanese Taverna. But I'm happy she likes her present! It is a beautiful, small Qom silk rug. As we talk about the best way to frame the rug, some part of my mind pays attention to nearby gunfire and the buzzing of the radio inside.

I worry that framing the rug might take away from its beauty. With a frame, won't the glass make it more difficult to see? I wonder if there is a way to have it mounted so that it can be put on the wall but without enclosing it in glass or having an actual frame around the borders. I think about the rug's uniqueness;

when viewed from different angles, different colors and designs emerge. Without glass, I think she could view it from its different sides without getting a reflection. Perhaps I could make something that can hold the rug from its corners (like a clamp) and thus allow it to be hung freely so you can periodically change the side that the rug is hung from (long way, short way, etc.). . . .

Why in the hell am I thinking about the many ways to hang a rug?

Tomorrow—wait, it's today, I realize as I look at my watch—we will head out on patrol, to go over to the Iraq police station, and it's very possible, perhaps even likely, that we will chance on an IED and one of us will be killed. And then tonight, I'll be in a cell and from the corner I'll hear a wail and I'll wonder "is this a killer, or does an innocent suffer?" Rugs, really? So I end my short talk with Amy and head inside the TOC and take a quick glance at my watch: 3 A.M.? Several more hours until my shift is over. I rest my booted feet on the table. I lean back. I stare at the ceiling. This time by myself in the TOC is actually enjoyable.

I am getting frustrated with the Americans I work with, and I just do not want to be around them anymore. Sometimes I want to stop interacting with Iraqis too, but I want to avoid the Americans even more. It's hard to spend a year with the same nine people in such an austere, lonely, and isolated environment. After a while, we just all start to go our own separate ways. Now, it seems as if the only time I see another American on our base is if we have a required meeting, which is rare; if we go on patrol; or if I catch a glimpse of them in the distance as I talk with the Iraqis. There is one other American who also spends some time with the Iraqis, but everyone else seems to have disappeared, stopped talking, stopped interacting. It seems we all have personal habits and routines that work to keep us away—from each other, and from the Iraqis we are supposed to mentor. But these habits also work to keep us sane. When we are together, we seem to always argue, so we work to stay apart, to stay alone—we are each the

Lost Platoon in *Apocalypse Now*, only in microcosm. Is this a human adaptation to war?

One American seems never to leave his room, and he plays video games and sleeps, always sleeps, in his dark cave. Another soldier has several feral cats that he loves. He feeds them, plays with them, hugs them, and kisses their wet, pink noses. Another has bought a BB gun and prowls the grounds shooting little birds and the wild dogs that hide in the thick grass along the riverbank. Another is having an affair over the Internet. He tries to protect himself by closing the e-mails on our shared computer in the TOC; he knows our wives and girlfriends talk with his wife. But he sometimes forgets when he goes to the bathroom, and so we look at the screen and see him talking dirty to a girl in one chat session, while he writes an e-mail to his wife in another.

But I am sure that the other Americans are frustrated with me, too. This team was a hastily cobbled together group, and we all come from very different military jobs and personal backgrounds, and I imagine they think I am a typical Special Forces asshole—too special for his own good, who never talks with them but who is always talking with Iraqis. I guess when you are with the same people for so long in such a god-awful environment, even Mother Teresa could start to seem like a bitch.

Every tenth day is a day off, thank God. There are ten Americans on our team and so every day is someone's day off. On my day off I escape to my room—my refuge—where I watch movies (sometimes I'll binge-watch an entire series: the *X-Files*, or *24*)—and drink little airplane bottles of alcohol the whole time. I actually watched an entire season of *24* in 24hrs. But what do I really like? I like chick flicks, because I'm no longer able to see love, happiness, and sophomoric life difficulties. And I cry, every time, no matter the movie. Sometimes I think I watch movies just so I can cry.

Germany, September 2011

19 Days Remain

As Ernst and I talk about war, we quickly find common ground. He smiles, and I smile back.

"Where?" Ernst asks.

"What?" I answer.

"I asked if you've been to Iraq."

I nod a "Yes," then mention a few of the other places as well.

It is amazing how perceptions suddenly change, again, once we identify some similarities, some commonalities. Not the places we have been, or even our professions, which barely overlap, but with the things that we sense the other may have seen, may have experienced that are similar to our own memories.

Maybe it's the unusual week I just had. Or maybe it's this very unusual morning. Maybe it's the long life I see scratched in the corners of his eyes. I don't know why, but for some reason, at this moment, on this hotel porch, on this Sunday morning, I feel something I have never felt before: I look at him and I don't want to take his truth. I want him to tell me his story, and not for any selfish personal reason. I want to *feel* him.

"It was 1939," he begins. "I was one year old then.

"I was a German living in Poland. My father told our family that Hitler left no doubt about the invasion and that we must leave in a hurry. If we didn't, he said, we would all be killed. So we left and we fled to Turin, where we were considered German refugees. Then in 1940 the first Allied planes came. I was two years old then. I think it was the Fiat factories in the city that brought the bombs. Our family moved again, this time to Dresden.

"It took us many weeks, but we finally made it to Dresden, where we spent five hard years. I had a big family with lots of relatives in the city, and we were sometimes hungry, but we were also very happy.

"Then when I was seven, in 1945, I remember hearing the planes; it seemed as if thousands of planes came over the city. To a young boy, those planes were so exciting and they seemed to fill the sky and I remember looking up and being thrilled. Then the fires began. In three days, everyone I knew, all my family, everyone was dead. Only I survived.

"That's when I turned eight. It took weeks, but I walked north to Berlin. Then the Soviets started the shelling. I remember seeing Soviet soldiers running in the city, and others grabbed me and we ran west hoping to meet Americans or maybe the British; anyone, just not the Soviets. That was a hard month, but I survived. Several years later, in 1949, the new German government said I had to take a job caring for British soldiers who were living in Germany.

"Then I turned eleven. I was to be their handy man, the fixer, and I'm not even sure there is a name for the job I do. But I have done this work every day since then. I retired a few years ago. I was just getting too old. I have no family, but I'm here today with friends because today is my birthday. Today, I turn seventy-two."
He smiles.

"How could you have done this?" I ask him. "How could you, for so long, have dedicated your life to the same people, the same cause that killed your entire family?"

He stares back at me and takes a second to respond. "It became good. Now, the Germans, the Brits, and the Americans, are like this," he says as he clasps his hands together. "We are friends."

I touch his hand and look Ernst in the eye, and I tell him: "It doesn't matter how wrong the Nazis were, we were also wrong for Dresden. I know it was a long time ago, but I want to say I'm really sorry."

Ernst raises his hands to his mouth, looks away, and then turns back to me. His hands now hide a face that is reddening, and his eyes begin to glisten, swelling, and I realize he is trying not to cry. He coughs. And then he starts to cry . . . and I can feel him. I sense his tired heart beating faster, his chest struggling, rising and falling, and I hear his shallow breathing, and I know now that he has been waiting a long time to share this pain with someone willing to truly listen, who wanted to understand. I squeeze his hand and on this porch, surrounded by Germans and a sunrise over grapevines on a Sunday morning, we cry together. This old man and me.

Is this the reason I've been changing? Was this God's hand on my shoulder saying "The horror had a purpose. You are ready. Take a step. Truly attend to the moment"?

Everything is starting to make sense—every choice in my life led to this moment where at 9:32 A.M. on a Sunday morning on a hotel porch in Germany, I would be the exact person who could hear an old man's inside whisper. He didn't know he needed this, but I somehow chose to become the person that was able to extend a hand.

However, the rational man hidden inside senses a faint crack in this tidy façade as I sit on the bench with Ernst: "These are not the musings of a sane man. You are in rapture, forever falling away from redemption . . . be careful."

Iraq, 2005

280 Days Remain

"You cannot allow the terrorist to sit and be the same as the interrogator," he answers. "Do whatever you can to create divisions within the group."

We're on a small break after an hour of endless interrogating and now Saedi is talking, again. Tonight we are interrogating a group whom we put together in a single cell. These guys are such assholes. I hate them.

But "asshole" is such a soft word. Asshole is for the boss, the obnoxious friend, the stranger in the grocery-store line whose credit card won't work. Most adjectives are not derogatory enough. I could call them terrorists, but this word is so overused that it's become a cliché. Insurgents? Nope. The media has turned that word into a "fighter for a just cause." So I'll just call them killers, or murderers, or criminals, because there isn't an English word that captures their evil.

". . . Like today," Saedi continues, "we put these guys in one cell. Do you want to go talk with them? I think they are about ready."

Shit, my mind was wandering. "Na'am," I respond, hoping I was right.

I slowly rise out of my metal chair to go and take a short walk to the room where they are being held, and all the while Saedi provides some background.

"We know that Mohammed is involved in a kidnapping operation where he and his brother Ahmed are partners. They captured, tortured, used, and then killed this young girl, who was the daughter of the local Muktar. They were trying to get money from the Muktar and to force him to oppose the Americans. Then we brought in Mohammed's son, Adel, and confronted him with the information we know, the things we know that Mohammed and Ahmed did. But instead, we accused Adel of kidnapping this girl, having sex with her, and killing her. Of course, he denied this because he didn't do it; we made him think that his father and uncle had told us he did. So we just left them all together in the same room to think, but the guard in the room didn't allow them to talk. They just sat and stared at each other; they get madder and madder as they think about what the other may have told us. It is fun to watch because really they have not told us anything at all." Saedi chuckles.

And then Saedi and I enter the room. It's quiet, and sitting on the floor are two men and a boy. A guard stands near the door, and I let Saedi enter first and then watch, incognito-like, from the corner, behind my black wool mask.

I can't understand the fast and complicated Arabic of this interrogation, but I catch a few easy words. I watch their body language, observe the arrangement of the room, the positions of all the people. I decide to move closer and sit next to Saedi, who is only a foot away from the group who sit on the cement floor. Sometimes when I stand close to a prisoner I feel their passions inside me: the fury, then their comradery with fellow killers; the hatred, then their love for a newborn son; and the mortal toil, then their supreme joy when the keepers say "Well have you done!

142

Enter. Dwell therein." These terrorists' emotions are a physical thing, and I'm addicted.

These interrogations are like movies: they are enlightening, depressing, and an obsession. It's as if I am driving slowly past a horrible auto accident and have some overwhelming compulsion to look, but I also feel a sense of guilt. I pretend to keep my head straight, but I look out from the corner of my eye. I try to understand my compulsion, but I can't explain it completely. Do these interrogations pull back curtains that conceal a truth we hide from the world? Sometimes when I witness a confession, I imagine a hidden door creaking open . . . but I have to take a peek. I have to look; it's the room where our secret souls hide in the dark.

And when I do, I catch a glimpse of the real people within. And I see divisions that we create between them. I see the motivations that we shake loose. Like these men who sit here, only a foot away, who sit face to face . . . I can sense them.

Then I hear Saedi say to the father of Adel: "But your son remembers the girl he captured and killed from al-Arabiya neighborhood. Why don't you?"

The son shouts "No! It was not me but him who had sex with her," as he points to his uncle. "He had sex with her and then killed her with two rounds in the head."

"Yes," responds the father, "but you had sex with her also." Then he tells the son, "But you are the one who threw her into the river."

Adel yells back at his father, "But you were the one who raped the other girl!"

"Another girl?"

Fuck. I now see the logic of this technique. Instinctually righting a perceived wrong is more important than each man's instinct to protect himself, even more powerful than the bond between father and son. And now I know more than what I was confirming. There is another girl, and I wonder what became of her. I imagine she's a tiny thing, and I feel her cowering and crying on some cold floor. She has blood on her thighs and I'm crying inside because soon we'll find her body in some alley.

But these killers' emotions got the better of them and in their haste they impulsively and accidentally confessed. Dumb fucks. I hope we will find her, but I know this hope only makes me feel better. More than likely, we will never know what happened to her.

I feel my hate, so I look to Saedi. I give him a slight nod. He nods in return. I stand up from my corner of the room.

I leave the shadows.

To enter the light.

I walk over to the father.

I step in close, only inches from his face.

As the Iraqi guards hold his shoulders, I reach out and wrap my fingers around his neck: he deserves the justice a raped and dead girl cannot give him. . . .

I begin to squeeze and I feel the heart beat, faster, as my grip becomes tighter, and eventually the struggling, breathing, and then thinking slows, and quietly the world becomes one person-less better. I actually sense the shift, which is not a thing-in-itself. I just know the scales have changed, for a balanced equation is a moral obligation. It feels good, this doing something . . .

. . . "No, no," Saedi answers, and I'm pulled back from my wishful thinking. My mind was wandering, and I was only imagining that joyful neck-squeezing. My eyes refocus and my heart slows . . . I look around and realize we are now sitting in his office after the confessions.

"The lesson here is one of pride and of saving face," he continues. "They don't care about hurting themselves as long as they can get back at the other, to hurt the other even more. But this technique does not always work. Many times, terrorists will confess in the hope that a confession will save them.

"I remember a terrorist named Issam. Issam was engaged, so we told him 'Your brother is gone, he is a terrorist—and the same goes for your nephew. They kidnapped that boy and used him and then killed him. So you now have to save yourself. Why? Because your brother and nephew gave you up. But I know they made you do these things and you also have your new wife. You have a future. If you talk with us, I will write in my investigation that you helped us. The maximum you will stay in jail is three months.' So then he started to give me a few short confessions. I told him, 'This is useless,' and I raised my arm and pretended to hit him. I told him, 'I will cut off your penis and then release you and you can then go to your wife as a female.' I had my assistant start to take off the prisoner's pants. The prisoner cried, and squirmed, desperate to confess. So we sit him down on a chair, give him a cigarette and some chai, and show him respect as I have a soldier type up a confession that I hope will get him many years in prison.

"Mr. Bill, if they are afraid, they always convince themselves that I am telling the truth. The fear they create within themselves is more powerful than anything I could do." "And if an innocent person confesses?" I ask. "It happens. But usually I will find out," Saedi replies. "And remember, Mr. Bill, even innocent people have information that can stop terrorism."

It is 1 A.M. and I just got off the phone with Amy; I woke her up to tell her I love her, and how yesterday was a busy day. I went on patrol. I was the gunner.

I try to describe to Amy how on the way home, I push the traffic, the smell of burning trash, and the roving car bomb to the back of my mind and close my eyes, to let go and escape the moment . . . I transport myself far away to feel the wind on my face and the sun escape into my eyes and to hear the leaves slide across a special trail. I smell the fresh scent of pine as my heart beats in time with the rise and fall of my knees. I pull deep breaths and fill my chest with air and then I look up, way, way up, above me to the beautiful summit and I see the miles of switchbacks slide from side to side that disappear in to the clouds. Back on earth, a bird flies close by my eyes and I take another deep breath. I swell my chest and I feel my toes grab the earth as I glide forward, moving left and right, up and down over rocks and roots. My legs become heavy and I begin to slow and my heart starts to ache so I adjust my form, minutely, and then I refocus and I lift my mind from the trail, which is just under my toes, to see the trees that are farther away and the curve in the trail before it reaches the next switchback. Soon I will reach the overlook that is just up ahead, and I focus on the next place ahead of me. My mind expands as I surge, glide, and float. I feel at one with the mountain, with the river valley, with myself and the world. This trail where I run is such a beautiful place and I know I must return here more often, at least in my mind, so I can lose myself on Pike's Peak Barr Trail, my favorite running trail . . . then I feel my body lean to the right as we swerve left around a suspiciously parked car, and I'm back in Mosul. Our front tire crashes into a water-filled pothole and drops of sewage fly through the air to splash on my face and a few drops perch at the corners of my mouth, and one drop slowly finds its way inside to land on my tongue, and . . . Fuck! . . . I reflexively spit and my eyes flash open to check that my finger lies comfortably ready on the side of my trigger . . . I scan, right and then left . . . but now I smile.

~

I look toward the horizon and even the faint light of the morning sun hurts. I need more time for my eyes to adjust after the darkness of the prison.

There is beauty in these early-morning hours. The town is always peaceful this time of day; from every direction the only sound I hear are calls to prayer. These calls seem to echo off the cliffs on the far-side riverbank, and Saedi and I walk over to stand under a tall tree to talk. We just stand there next to the river.

There is a fence with mounds of razor wire between us and the river, but we still get as close to the water as we can. I like to just stare at the Tigris flowing by.

As Saedi blows smoke, I admire the view and I look to the far bank to see the oldest part of Mosul's downtown. Under the morning light I can see the outline of rooftops and get a hint of the highest windows, where perch a generation of satellite dishes. I'm reminded of Pristina, Kosovo, where there were so many dishes we called it the polka dot city.

I slowly move my view down to just under the city's sky-line, and I see the narrow streets where just above car height are millions of electrical wires and power cords and television cables that stretch from pole to pole and crisscross the roads from side to side. There are so many of these wires over the roads, some old and some new, and many of them unused, that sometimes when we are on patrol I will look up and these cords form a spider web so dense that in places they almost black out the sky.

And then on the far riverbank my eyes move lower down from the street to see the bits and pieces of an even older city—old ruins, and walls, and in some places old bricks jutting out from the mud. And then lower down, right at the water's edge, are the flats where daily I watch some farmer eking out a living by grazing a few old goats or one grungy lamb. Down to the left, along the bank, I see a small boat pushed halfway into the tall grass.

I sometimes worry that an infiltrator will use this side of our perimeter to paddle a boat across in the middle of the night to bring in a gun, a bomb, or suicide vest, and I ask myself "Should I worry about that small boat that I see sticking out from the grass?" At the same time, I notice, just above the boat, a patrol of Strykers exiting slowly from a too-narrow city street. There are three Strykers, all in a row, and I think of those soldiers who are continuously on patrol and consistently dying. Now my mind is no longer wandering, I am no longer imagining, so I turn back from the bank and ask

Saedi if we can continue walking—this is probably a good time for some more questions.

"Saedi, can you tell me about Zubayr, the killer we just finished interrogating?"

"We knew Zubayr was a strong terrorist," he tells me. "I know that he is a smuggler of weapons; smugglers of weapons are very brave. He had been captured before and tortured by Saddam's Economy Security. But I have only a few days to break someone, so I do not waste my time or energy on Zubayr. I must focus on the weak ones. I must focus on the weak, the young, those I already have information on, the relatives. I use these people to quickly move to the next house with a terrorist and to other members of the strong one's cell. You pull a loose string in a rug, and the whole rug will come apart. So besides Zubayr, we have three other terrorists from his cell: Mufid, Mu'in, and Nash'ah. Nash'ah was the son of Mufid, and Mu'in was Mufid's brother. Many times you capture fathers and sons and family members. I started with Nash'ah.

"First, he was young, so he will be scared quickly, and also he can be lied to and manipulated easily. First, we told him, 'You are young. You are under the legal age. We will never execute you, even if you killed a thousand. They will keep you in a jail for two years at a special jail for rehabilitation.' And then we told him that his father is now gone. We refuse his request to go see his body. 'It is better that one is lost and one confesses so he can go home,' we tell the young one. 'If not, then both of you will be killed.' He told me a few things, about how they captured a boy to get money from a father and how his father and his father's friends then dumped the body. And then I told him, 'I know this, and this, and this. There is more. I know you lie to me! Take him to be tortured.' He starts to cry and begs to confess."

"So how do you identify this weak one, terrorists like Nash'ah?" I ask.

"First are the poor, then the young, then I go after the one in the cell who did the least number of operations—this is usually the least

148

important person—and I go after him. For the young person, the best thing to do is to scare him and then you take good care of him.

"I once had a twelve-year-old and he was crying. He kept saying he wanted to go home to his mommy. We cared for him, gave him chips and cigarettes, but did not let him go to his mom. After two days, he told me about his father. 'Three Mujahideen came to my home,' he said. 'My father is a Mujahideen. I bring out chai and these men, I hear them talking about killing our neighbor because he works with the Americans. One man gives me a thousand dinar when he comes to my home, and when he pulled the money out of his pocket, I saw an American identification card fall out of the pocket. They left the house. After an hour, my neighbor was dead. We called the mother and had her pick up her dead son.'

"You see?" says Saedi. "This boy was the weak link that led me to a group; weak by body language, by his look, and his age. But age is never the perfect sign. Some of the worst terrorists are very young and some are even very old. Once I focused my efforts on the poor old man of a large group and when confronted by the basic facts that sources had already told us, of the IEDs he planted and Americans they shot at, he gave us a lot of information about the entire group. So we captured the group and from that point I chose who I thought was the next weakest person and confronted him with the information obtained from the first. Over a three-day period using this method and basic mental and physical pressure, five of the nine confessed."

"Were they all guilty?" I asked.

"Yes. They confessed, didn't they? We made them miserable so that finally they decided to tell us the truth. But we could get this information faster if we were allowed to use harder techniques. Now, I think that because we are soft on these terrorists, more Iraqis will die and they will just be released from prison once we turn them over to the Iraqi police."

"Saedi, you know we can't," I reply, but I also think that I just don't care.

If these men talk, an innocent will be saved and who would ever know how we attained the information? It's the positive result that matters. Really. I feel stuck between two bad choices and I must decide which choice is the worse. Do I protect a terrorist who kills and rapes and as a consequence risk not getting the intelligence that will save another innocent, an Iraqi or maybe even an American? By not allowing "harder" interrogation techniques, do I risk not getting a confession so that when these killers are turned over to the Iraqi police they will just eventually be released, only to kill again? But damn it! What about the mistakes, the few "killers" who we learn are just victims of Iraqi vendettas?

"Mr. Bill. No one would ever know. We would not leave marks; and if we did, we would drive them north to Kurdistan and they would never be heard from again. We will be saving Iraqis."

"Saedi. No. I can't," I force myself to say, and then leave him standing beside the riverbank.

Germany, September 2011

19 Days Remain

I hear a low grating noise, the faint wisp of a last crackling exhalation . . . I keep my eyes shut, but still it gets louder and more persistent with each passing second until it is painfully deafening. I crack an eye open, just one, to register that I'm in the passenger seat of our Volvo SUV, and Cheryl, the girls, and I are driving home from the hotel after our camping trip. I now know that that sigh is the car's engine and that the conversation I had with Ernst was yesterday, and was real. Yet Cheryl is scared.

She sees that I am becoming more and more unhinged, and she doesn't understand why. But I do: she can't see the suffering that I've caused. But still she is concerned about me, and more importantly she is troubled about what my slide means for our family. She is right to fear. I sit here in the passenger seat with a blank look on my face, while my mind races and jumps from thought to thought to thought. It is as if my brain has become a huge mob, screaming and scattering in every direction, with no sense, no reason, just bumping and careering in every direction.

I am out of control; and now that I am awake, I am talking to Cheryl at a thousand miles an hour and she moves from scared to terrified.

"Bill. Just lie back," she says. "Close your eyes. Take a deep breath and focus on control."

I lie back and my thoughts ricochet off each other; my mind is running a million miles an hour. I close my eyes. I try to breathe deeply, to focus on control, but instead I start thinking: about what, and why, I just don't fucking know . . . but I can see that language is confining. My thoughts, they are confusing, my words make no sense, and I realize that combining twenty-six letters in different configurations between spaces does not allow for infinite variation. Language is limiting and confining. I feel trapped, alone inside of my mind.

But then a flash. Of course!

Everything makes sense.

God found me. I am His Prophet.

Of course I'm thinking gibberish.

I am a mortal vessel translating the celestial.

I am feeble and imperfect, so of course His words are incomprehensible.

But I also feel I'm going insane, my thoughts tumbling forward, pushing reality—Cheryl and the girls—further and further away.

Iraq, 2005

259 Days Remain

My parents tell me they want to find a way to donate to a cause that supports soldiers. I'm glad to hear this, and I'm sending them a list of worthy organizations and websites. There is no shortage of places to donate. The real problem is that the voices that soldiers hear are the ones that are loudest: those who scream, who incite, inflame, who are controversial. Soldiers need to see that people *are* supporting them, because that's not what we see on television over here. We hear people say "I do not support the war, but I support the soldier." It's bullshit, really, and does not help take away our feeling of abandonment. This is how I felt when my parents went to San Francisco to attend a war protest. I know they make this distinction and that they love me, but it also made me angry. Really angry.

Last night we detained some young Iraqis—just kids, really, but still killers who murdered two innocent Iraqis—and I interrogated them. Will the protesters come over here to do these things, the same things they have asked me to do? Stop these people who are killing American soldiers and Iraqi civilians? No, they would not.

Yesterday, I played the driving version of Russian roulette—for the gazillionth time—and last night we were mortared, just a few rounds that landed on the base, but I have gotten used to this by now.

Last night when the rounds hit, it was late, and I just rolled over and went back to sleep. When I'm asleep, I just don't want to leave my room again, at least until I have to start a new day. For me to care enough to disturb my sleep, something really big has to happen. I have to literally feel the air pressure change from the force of an explosion and to feel the dust that's shaken loose from my ceiling touch my face. Only then would I roll out of bed. And if I am outside, I need to actually see the strike of the bullet, to see the dust lift from the ground around my feet, to hear the snap of the bullet breaking the sound barrier near my head; only these things would raise my heart rate. I just don't seem to care anymore, and it's scary to think about how un-scared I have become.

Will the war protester understand? Do they even care? I doubt it. This war was a choice; and when a choice is easy, choices are repeated easily and then easily forgotten. We are forgotten, and waving signs assuages guilty consciences. But then again, waving a sign is at least doing something. I should despair when I no longer see a protest, when we become indifferent.

⌒

I've noticed an improvement in my relationships with Iraqis since I have been speaking Arabic. But the Kurds speak Kurdish and they hate Arabic, the language of one of their many oppressors. This is especially true for Saedi. I'm sometimes astonished at how racist everyone is. Many of them absolutely hate Arabs, even to the point of hating the Arabic language. But there are some who do not have this feeling. Many of the Kurdish officers are college-educated and so help me to speak Arabic properly. Many times, however, I will ask a Kurd how to say a word in Arabic and he will trick me and tell me the answer in Kurdish. Most of the time I can tell that the word is Kurdish, but sometimes I am fooled and memorize the Kurdish word until an interpreter asks "Why do you mix Kurdish and Arabic?"

Hashim, my elderly Arabic interpreter, is my primary teacher. When he teaches me, he spends half the time talking theology. It's fascinating to learn about Islam from a Muslim, a true Muslim, not the fanatics that I interrogate, and to hear his perspective about his own religion. I love to hear his perspective about Iraq, the world, about terrorists, and even about Christianity. But sometimes I want to tell him to just stop, to not talk about these heavy things; I just want to focus on the language, to lose myself in the beautiful right-to-left flow as each word is artfully formed. The Arabic language is beautifully logical, which is calming. But sometimes Hashim's tangents strike a chord, which disrupts the meditative flow of words and snaps me back to reality.

Hashim teaches how similar, inclusive, and accepting both Islam and Christianity really are. "Mr. Bill," he tells me, "the teachings of Mohammed—'alayhi as-salām—and the words of Allah demand that Muslims respect Jews and Christians because all believe in God." The primary difference between Muslims and Christians, Hashim tells me, is the prophet we follow: "there is no god but the God, and Mohammed is the Prophet of God," Hashim teaches, and he believes Christians think the same, except that Christ is our Prophet. Hashim doesn't think that justifies the hatreds between us. One of the main points of Muslim terrorists, Hashim says, is their belief that Jews and Christians are "unbelievers." But he makes the point—with a finger punching to the sky—that the Koran and the teachings of the Prophet Mohammed explicitly state that Christians and Jews are believers. Hashim says that this is one of the largest lies about Islam that the terrorists distort for their own twisted purposes.

Regardless of what Hashim teaches, living here makes me not want to believe in any prophet, or even in a god. God only gives people an excuse to do what they want. And looking at ourselves, I know the bad outweighs the good.

—

Last night when I spoke with Amy, I told her I am starting to take on the mannerisms of Iraqis: I find myself saying "the Americans" like they are somehow different than myself, which is unsettling.

And then there is this: Iraqis hold up a hand with the right thumb, index finger, and middle finger pulled together, touching, then they make a clicking sound. It seems this mannerism is to stress a point. I have observed that now, when I am talking, I sometimes do the same thing. I've even started to hold a man's hand as we walk, just like an Iraqi. What does she think about this? She never says.

Today was another busy day—prisoners coming and going, meetings, getting information on terrorists, etc., etc. Last night we caught a guy sneaking around the outside of the base. I tell her this too. Not a good sign, I say, because it presages an attack. I am just waiting for the time a car comes barreling through our front gate, past the Iraqis who half-heartedly guard this place. The building where I sleep is right on this car's path.

Germany, September 2011

19 Days Remain

"Hold him down. Mr. Bill, hold him down. Bill . . . Bill . . . we're almost home . . . Bill," says Cheryl as she reaches across to nudge my thigh. Cheryl is scared and we're almost home from our camping trip, and I am still thinking about holding shoulders to a floor. . . .

"Do you want to go to the hospital, or home?" she asks. I stay silent.

I want to believe in God, but I just can't. I need this, this hope, even though I hold no stronger conviction than that there is no God. Experience seems all the proof I need for this conviction. But then, just this morning, right before I spoke with Ernst, I'm suddenly converted? Me, a born-again Christian?

I'm conflicted, and this inner conflict is an electrical current that both hums and sizzles, and then the opposing currents meet inside of my brain. Please, someone help me because I'm absolutely certain God found me and yet I am also absolutely certain there is no such thing as a god. God, I am fucking insane. No, fuck god.

I see my struggle reflecting in Cheryl's eyes and right now, in the passenger seat, it is only Cheryl, looking at me with love and concern, that pulls me back from the edge of oblivion. I close my eyes, and I literally feel her love so I take a deep breath; I breathe it in. It sustains me. I close my eyes. I breathe again.

"Let's go home," I say as I close my eyes.

Iraq, 2005

251 Days Remain

It is mid-afternoon and I notice that new prisoners are arriving. "Tonight will be another long night," I say to myself as I walk back from talking with my interpreters in their room.

I put my hands behind my back and tongue the dip behind my lower lip. I turn my eyes skyward. The sun is glaring, and I can't help but wonder if the reflection off my bald head is a bullet's lure. Nevertheless, I am still enjoying my walk.

I'm thinking about religion and about God, who is seen from so many perspectives. There is no better place to learn about God than from killers who use God to justify their killing.

Most of our prisoners claim that religious beliefs and principles are the reason they fight. I am starting to see that this is bullshit. It seems that the insurgent rarely fights for religious reasons alone. Faith is almost never their primary motivation. Islam is the terrorist's public excuse. Usually the motive is far more selfish, whether it is greed, power, or just a grudge. But this does not imply that insurgents are not religious or that religion does not play an important role in defining who they are or how they act.

And, of course, religion is an effective recruitment device and means of control and manipulation. Religion is used by cell imams to pass judgments on kidnap victims or to bless an operation to ensure its success. Religion is used to entice the poor or sick with the possibility of a better life. It is used to incite the populace and to justify acts of terrorism. Here, the prospect of sex with a passel of virgins in Paradise will lure in a thousand lost, but also horny, men. Here, religion is the ultimate trump card and their violence is virtuous and not intended only for self-defense. *"Fighting is prescribed for you,"* says the Koran. Saedi knows this. In fact, he uses this to his advantage. I've come to admire the art of using a terrorist's own interpretations of God's words so that we can stop their killing.

Amy finally got her present, a Kurdish bracelet, and luckily I'm able to get an Internet connection so I can tell her about it. We chat about the mundane irritating little notes from Wells Fargo Bank, the house refinancing. Anything other than this dusty shithole.

I have been abnormally tired lately and have not been able to get up in the morning in order to exercise. I do not know if it is just lack of sleep, or if I have a nutrition deficiency, or if I am just a lazy piece of shit. Whatever the reason, I find myself turning off my alarm and not wanting to get up. I just want to roll over and go back to sleep.

We've had a sniper problem lately, and I've had a couple of close calls . . . yesterday morning I actually did manage to pry myself from my bed in the morning, and was running fast, enjoying the adrenaline. I rounded the corner of the dirt road that goes toward the end of my home and then I noticed a puff of dirt near my toes . . .

. . . then I hear a "crack" a second later. I fall down and then crawl to a nearby bush, the only bush around me, it seems. I stop and think "about 400 meters away." I then crawl to some large rocks and stay there for a while. After ten minutes I wonder if my mind is playing tricks on me, or is a sniper really trying to kill me? I decide it's all my imagination so I take a breath and stand up . . . nothing . . . so I walk back to our office. But I can't help but wonder if my time is now . . . and in slow motion I watch a bullet travel along its trajectory. Slowly it pushes the air forward and then my skin splits and bone parts like butter . . . nothing . . . which is fascinating to experience in slow and sterile detail. I write it off.

But then this morning it happens again as I am walking outside with Saedi.

I ask Saedi "What if I was a prisoner in your cell? How should I resist your interrogation?" Then we begin our slow walk around the base.

"Make me waste time," he says. "You remember Aziz? That terrorist who kidnapped those three students? The one who held them in the basement for a ransom but decided to just shoot them when getting money took too long? Yes, him. Well, Aziz at first gave a false name, so I could do nothing but focus on trying to get his real name and to try to get him to admit to who he really was. Ahhh! Make me focus on something small that has nothing to do with why you are here. Like a name. All other facts and considerations were irrelevant until I could prove who he was, and it was very frustrating.

"Then, if that is not working, try to act innocent and then always work to confirm this impression. Never rush your answers. Always think and then talk, but do this always, when you're both telling the truth and lying.

"Or if you want something that is even easier," he continues, "know in your mind that I know you are guilty, so focus on resistance and not talking. Don't try to convince me that you are innocent. Tell your story and don't change it. It does not matter if I know you are lying. As long as you do not confess, you will win. Do not be hostile. Make me work, and work, and work. Just say the same story no matter how stupid it may sound when I confront you with proof that you are lying. Do not believe anything I say, for lying is crucial for the interrogator to find your weakness and break your resistance. Every person has his own key to resistance. The trick for me is to find that one thing that gives you hope, and then when found, to suddenly take it away."

Saedi takes a moment to pull long and hard on a cigarette, and I realize we have only a hundred meters before we complete our loop.

Saedi blows smoke out of his nose before he continues. "If you do these things, you will make me believe that you will require too much effort and especially that you are not the weak one. The interrogator is usually busy. He has other duties and responsibilities and other detainees. To you, the prisoner, you think you are the most important thing in the world and that there is nothing more important than for me to focus my time and energy on making you talk. But this is not usually the case. You must realize that the chances are good that you are really not very important at all. Just another detainee, and the interrogator is trying to see if his time is well spent focusing on you versus someone else."

As the conversation ends, I look up and realize we've completed our circle of the base and we're standing outside the TOC. Then there is a SNAP!

The bang of a gun is boring, but the whip-like "SNAP" of a bullet breaking the sound barrier over your head is something else entirely. My heart rate actually rose—just a bit. Now, when having my "walk and talks" with Saedi, I vary the way I walk around the base.

⌒

Today is Sunday and another week is gone, but then another week begins and the cycle repeats. Shit, time just ticks and ticks, and every time I check it seems that no time has passed. It would probably be better if I just stopped keeping track, but then sometimes something happens that makes the passage of time less of a burden.

Saedi was instructing me on how insults are a good interrogation technique and then he tells me "To say 'You son of a bitch!' sometimes works, and it helps if you follow with a hard kick or slap. But if they are religious or Takfiri, cussing only shows them you do not respect God; so until you are better at speaking Arabic, don't insult or curse. You will just make mistakes and this will make things worse." Then we switch topics. That was yesterday.

Today, we are standing outside to the rear of his office building and we're leaning against the off-white stucco walls that face away from the bright midday sun. There is no wind and it's hot. I ask: "Saedi, I need you to put together a PowerPoint briefing about the terrorist cell from al-Sukar neighborhood. Can you do this? Can this briefing have all of the information that we just talked about today?"

The information I was referring to was a terrorist cell we hadn't previously known about. It was a Mortar Cell, a small cell that specialized in only lobbing mortars onto the American bases. They're not very effective, but man, are they annoying to Americans. I tell Saedi that putting together this briefing about this cell would be a very good way for the Americans to see the quality of the information that he gets. Saedi responds with an emphatic "Fuck your mother!" And he accentuates this with a raised hand, thumb, forefinger, and middle-finger touching, and a few verbal "clicks" with his tongue.

I couldn't believe it and got really upset. But then I took a breath, thought it through, and realized that he wouldn't have intentionally said what he just did, that this must have been a mistake. I then realized that his mistake was that he tried cussing in English, a language that he barely speaks. He was doing the very same thing that he warned me not to do. He hears American soldiers say "motherfucker!" and, because of the structure of the

Arabic language, he reversed the word order. He was trying to "stylishly" tell me he didn't want to do the work of a PowerPoint briefing for some Americans, which is time-consuming and which he thinks is a complete waste of his time.

I thought about this on my patrol this afternoon, and the memory brought on a smile.

We are having Internet problems again, so this afternoon we drove to the American base and I was finally able to connect with Amy. I talk to her about Saedi's Fuck Your Mother, answer her queries about petty money matters, reassure her that I know she is doing her best. I also tell her that Saedi is getting married. I won't make it to his wedding, but I will be able to get him a gift.

⌁

"Mr. Bill, do you know what the terrorists and even the people are saying? They say 'Even the Americans do not want the terrorists to go away from Iraq. The Americans put them in a nice jail, with food and beds, and after two or three months they will be released. We must make rules that fit our situation! In Texas, this state has execution, but maybe in Georgia they do not have executions. In Iraq we need this same right. We must have sentences that are fit for the times. We must have special terrorist courts. Now we must capture, investigate, interrogate in three days! Now, this is only serving the terrorists! Americans say 'This is an Iraqi decision, you have your own government.' The Iraqi government says 'This is the way,' but we know that the government makes no decision that the Americans do not want. I cannot even slap my own prisoner who I know rapes young girls and boys, kills people, and cuts off heads?! This is causing us to become weak and to not take responsibility! Why are there these rules for me?"

Saedi is angry, again, and today I am also angry at him.

Ten minutes ago I was in a smoke-filled cell and I stood in the back wearing my black wool mask. Saedi sat on a chair with his knees crossed. On a small metal table in the corner is an Iraqi soldier taking notes. The prisoner is on the floor, legs crossed, and his hands are in the air and he is wailing. We were there for what seemed hours.

"Where is she?" Saedi yells and points at the prisoner with two yellow nicotine-stained fingers. "Where is she?" he yells again. Then, from the corner of my eye, I see a quick movement and a left arm comes around and I hear the "crack" of a slap, a boot flies forward to lay a body on the floor, and then a knee presses down into the small of a back. Saedi calms down and walks behind the blindfolded man, who rises slightly to lean sideways. Saedi takes a slow puff from his cigarette, leans down to whisper in the prisoner's ear, and then he looks up. He looks toward me with a question in his stare.

I don't know if he can sense the thoughts I have behind my mask, but I am pissed. I stare straight back at him and I think: "You son of a bitch!"

I am pissed. I am pissed because of a slap to a killer? A man who is hiding a kidnapped Iraqi who may soon be dead if not dead already? No, I am not mad for the hit and kick. I am pissed because he crossed the line that we both agreed would not be crossed. I am pissed because Saedi is forcing me to decide. Do I stick to the words of my hard compromise? I must now decide if I am going to follow through with my threats.

I know deep down that this is an issue where I must stand firm. I must be direct about what I expect. If not, I will be taken advantage of. And a decision to tell about his slap and kick *will* hurt our relationship.

I hate that he has forced this on me. I hate that I must care about a slap and kick to a piece of shit who deserves it. But I also know that the relationship I have with Saedi is critical and that our rapport is how I am both able to capture terrorists and simultaneously prevent their abuse. If I punish this small slap and kick to this killer, will I lose the influence that prevents real torture in the future? But I also think that if I stop a small slap or a kick to this killer, will this man not confess, and then will he just be released to soon rape and kill some more? If I report Saedi's transgression, he will get in trouble, he will lose face, and less importantly to him, but important to me, he may lose his job.

If Saedi is fired, where will I be? A new Iraqi intelligence officer will come in who is more like the majority that I now see, the Iraqi officer who just smokes and drinks chai while waiting for the promised wad of American dollars. Damn, I hate that we reward incompetence with hard-earned American taxpayer money. But on this small Iraqi base, this is not the case.

I am immensely lucky to work with an Iraqi who is both competent and hardworking, and I know that our partnership stops killers and saves innocent lives. If I report this slap and kick, where will we be then? Should I just start looking the other way, or must I do something? I am torn because I feel the same emotions that he does, the same emotions that precipitated this argument between us. And I not only want to hit and to slap, but sometimes I want to hurt, to kill these killers. I'm not sure what to do. . . .

Germany, September 2011

19 Days Remain

A "tell me!" is followed by a slap.

"There is a hidden room," he admits as legs shake. "He's in the basement." He cries and then wipes an eye above a pool of piss, and then; "The boy's inside." But I'm not fooled by your piss and tears. There's no human in there. I don't want your confession. What I need is for you to just . . . disappear. But I'm a good person, and I need the strength to overcome my weakness . . .

. . . Cheryl squeezes my shoulder . . . my eyes open and I realize we're home from the weekend camping trip, so I jump out of the car, leaving her to unpack and get the girls inside. I run in the house to write a quick e-mail about some thoughts, thoughts that I suddenly had on the drive home. . . .

From: Bill
To: askthemathematician@gmail.com

Hello,
I am not a mathematician so I have to ask my question using words.
My gut tells me that there are conditions where it is mathematically

possible for a circle to equal a straight line; for two completely different things to really be just the same thing. If I am correct in these equations, my belief tells me that it is possible for ($y=mx+b$) to equal $(X-H)^2 + (Y-K)^2=r^2$? Is this true or false? Has this been asked and answered before? Thanks, Bill

Iraq, 2005

238 Days Remain

Amy says, insistently, "I am out of deposit slips!"

I tell her that I do not have a way to get her a deposit slip. She has my fucking power of attorney, so she has control over my finances; ordering more checks should be simple, just call the bank and ask them. Why does she need me to solve this? I'm here making the money that she is living off of, so deal with it. Really, I don't need this fucking shit.

I give up and hang up.

Outside it is raining, the first big rain of the season. I hear the pounding and clanking of rain on some metal sheeting on the roof.

The wall next to my bed is now just plywood boards, so periodically I get a sprinkle of water on my face. My bedroom glass-less window now holds only an old clanking air-conditioner which used to be surrounded by sandbags that provided some protection from an explosion. But I took the sandbags out; it seemed that with every explosion I would wake up in the morning to find dust and dirt covering my face, which was definitely annoying.

But how the rain is beautiful; I love waking up to a clean smell, wet ground, and high winds blowing the tree tops. A night's rain is the perfect way to start a new day. It's renewing.

Today is the start of Ramadan. We are waiting to see the effect this holiday has on the fighting in the town, but here on this base we have trouble, big trouble right here in River City.

Since Ramadan is the month of fasting, there will be no eating, smoking, or drinking from 5:30 A.M. to 6:00 P.M. So everyone eats, smokes, and drinks all night long to get their day's worth of cravings over with before the start of the next day's fast. And then all day long everyone stays inside and usually sleeps. It's fitting that Ramadan's schedule matches with the interrogation—cravings are for the dark, and then use the day's light to sleep it off.

I am working hard on my Arabic and can now read proficiently. I have a little notebook where I keep all my translated words. In this book I will write, for example, "To talk = *yatakellam.*" Though I can now read Arabic, so far my memorization is purely by phonetic spelling, which has its drawbacks. There are at least four letters in the Arabic language that do not have a corresponding English sound. So inevitably I will mispronounce words. I know I need to move away from phonetic memorization, so today as the Iraqis sleep I head to my roof and for five hours rewrite my phonetic notebook.

Every English word now has its Arabic translation and it's written in Arabic. This way, I am forced to read the Arabic word to know how to pronounce it. I am up to about three hundred words so far. In maybe two more months I will not need a translator. I hope. And I know this will definitely help out with my long discussions with Saedi. If I can speak Arabic proficiently, even though Saedi dislikes the language, the time our conversations take will be cut by three quarters, something I am sure Saedi will enjoy.

Everyone here is gearing up for the constitutional referendum, and I'm excited and nervous to see how events unfold in the next few weeks. The consensus is that most Iraqis will vote and that the constitution will pass. The Iraqis who I work with think that if the constitution passes, everything will start to get better. They see this as the start of a new beginning. I hope so. But on the reverse side, the terrorists will also use this time of hope to spread panic and chaos. They think of this as the time to kill more, showing civilians how the government is ineffectual and cannot provide for their security. I hope not. And Saedi is always upset that he can't be tougher on the prisoners. "But you have the death penalty," he always says. "You are not Iraqi," he says. "You don't understand our ways," he says. "These human rights just ensure that terrorists go free and more innocent Iraqis are killed," he says. "You remember when we brought in that large group and made them all sit together with sandbags over their heads? Half we must set free because I couldn't prove a thing. These terrorists don't deserve any human rights," he says. "You are a soft American," he says. It is hard to argue against his logic, so now I just stay silent, but the argument takes place anyway. Saedi is determined, and the terrorists keep coming in. But I'm starting to feel that his terrorists are my "terrorists," likely killers but possibly . . . innocent? The pressure never goes away. I hope my hope stays with me. I hope.

~

It is Monday night, and tonight I stand outside the Iraqi mess hall and talk with a group of about fifteen Iraqi soldiers. Every hand holds a cigarette or a small cup of chai. In Arabic, "chai" means "tea," so when Americans ask for chai tea, our request is actually redundant. I like to imagine a long line of patrons at the local Starbucks in D.C., and as each customer arrives at the counter to place an order from a cute little doe-eyed barista, they proceed to make an innocent request: "Good morning. Can I have some TeaTea?"

As fifteen Iraqi males look at me strangely, I shake my grin away and restart our conversation: I'm explaining the American concept of dating. First, I tell these Iraqi jundees that we go out to places in order to meet someone. Our first hope is of getting lucky so you can go home and have sex. If not, then we exchange numbers in order to agree on a prearranged time and place to meet, to have a meal, and then hopefully to go home and have sex.

"Yes, guys pay for the meal," I tell them, but to them it always seems we are paying for sex. Then I tell them we go on a few more dates, to see if we are sexually compatible and if the other person is marriage material. Then we live together as a final test to see if the other is lifelong companionable. Then we marry, have kids, and then live happily ever after—at least that is our script. But I feel ridiculous trying to explain our sexual rituals; these guys barely even look at a woman until they are married, which I sense is unhealthy. Almost every interrogation uncovers some form of sexual torture, so I can't help but feel that forbidding the natural creates these perversions.

⌐

"Mr. Bill. Leaders are strong, but I have ways to make them talk; if I use electricity on him, he would confess in a half hour. But now I am not allowed."

"But what if the prisoner you torture is not guilty?" I ask.

"Yes, if I torture someone, he sometimes confesses to things he did not do. But these are only a few cases. But you must make sure you have enough information already. You check to see if his confession is the same as you already know. If so, then in this way we make sure he is put in jail."

It's hard not to critique this, but somehow I keep my silence— in Iraq, using torture to prove both a negative and a positive is logical and justified.

"But if you do not know something already," he continues, "then you must check what this person has said with your sources.

Like Ammar, in the interrogation this morning. Why did you not allow us to use the mother?"

"Saedi," I respond, "it's wrong to use a person's mother. She is innocent."

"Really?" he says. "Maybe she is not guilty but she has information. In our society, a woman probably does not agree with the man's job, but she knows what he does. Even a terrorist's wife is still a female. Females are like captives, and have no control, and have no responsibility or guilt. But they are good for information. On raids, we give soldiers the job of talking with the wife. The soldier will yell so everyone hears: 'Your husband is a terrorist and a killer of women and children!' Afraid, embarrassed, and weak, the wife will usually speak to this soldier."

"I understand this," I say. "But you use an innocent person to break a guilty person and then you are sometimes nice to the guilty person?"

"Sometimes we are really nice to a prisoner," says Saedi. "From one minute to the next, you give the terrorist a cigarette and drink of water, and then you hurt him. The terrorist is always trying to cheat, and he changes in his mind from one minute to the next. When we give him a smoke and tea, he believes that he is fooling the interrogator and that in thirty minutes the investigation will be over. And then we hit him. In his mind, this tells him 'Hey, we have you, we will not let you go, and don't ever think you understand us or what will happen next.' So from then he will fear, always on pins and needles, always careful. With that kind of stress, mistakes are inevitable. From then on, the cigarette is a reward without the terrorist getting the mental boost of thinking he has the upper hand. Hope should be just a glimmer, always there but just out of reach. They must see it, but then you must take it away; but do it slowly, unpredictably, and little by little. If they lose all hope, then there is little benefit to confess."

"So they talk because you keep them off balance," I ask, "and you—"

"This doesn't work with the professionals," Saedi says, cutting off my question. "The terrorist who is a fundamentalist and who you do not have months to interrogate: How do you get them to talk? First you need information on this person and a long time to interrogate. Then combined with physical and physiological pressure, he will break. Sometimes, when I have time, I will have someone very knowledgeable about religion come and speak with the terrorist only about the right and wrong of actions. You remember that prisoner who we knew was in charge of a cell that plants IEDs? If I had more time to interrogate, religious arguments would have worked. But instead he didn't confess and when we turned him over to the police they just let him go.

"So you see, if you do not have information already," Saedi continues, "and if you do not have time for a long interrogation, then pressure does not often work on a leader. They are too strong. In the past, I sometimes have put them in a very bright room, or I tie them up under a pipe and put a plate on his head. Let the water drip on this plate; slow but constant drips. Oh, this works very well. Soon, it is like a gun going off every second in your brain. Make a person very comfortable in a room with a nice bed, give him a shower and warm blankets, but then when he falls asleep on the bed, you shock him with cables from a car battery. Soon, you never have to do anything and he still is constantly stressed. During Saddam, we had to use these methods. Pretending to drown a prisoner, and a drill to here, the side of the knee, also works very well. Or when it is really hot you put him in a place that is very tight, a small space where he can never stand but also cannot sit. But remember, you must also be nice. Going from comfort to terror to comfort, then terror, over and over again; soon even the strongest will give in."

Germany, September 2011

17 Days Remain

I want the answer to my math inquiry. I can't explain it, but I feel that I'm on to something, something that explains the inexplicable. I'm anxious, this waiting, but it works very well and soon it is like a gun going off every second in my brain because I am comfortable in a room with a nice bed and warm blankets . . .

. . . and I'm restless, this waiting for the reply from the mathematician.

I don't know why I care so much, yet for some reason I just know that a circle is the same thing as a line. How we all, in our infinitely flawed ways, are trying, and trying, and trying again to learn to speak so we can understand how unhappiness is just misunderstandings. How we are trying to understand how different judgments of two objects are explanations of the same reality. How the reality of the universe is the same thing that someone else may call the Truth, Love, or God. How humanity's eternal squabbles about their different interpretations between right and wrong, faith and science, morality and utility, good and evil, male and female, 1 and 0, A and not-A, are, in fact, our diverse and perverse way of communicating our imperfect understandings about a perfectly true universe. I know if I prove this, if I uncover these hidden truths, then everything will make sense again. If a circle equals a line, then I will be fine. I just know it . . . and then the reply arrives. . . .

From: askthemathematician@gmail.com
To: Bill

Answer:

A circle can never be a straight line, though as you make the circle bigger and bigger its edge will look straighter and straighter. An ellipse, on the other hand, will basically be a line segment when its length along one axis goes to zero.

The Mathematician

From: Bill
To: askthemathematician@gmail.com

Another quick question and thanks for the quick reply! I have a second inquiry and please excuse me if it is a stupid one. And a one word "No" is OK :) I will understand.

If I were to change my perspective from a comparison between a two-dimensional object (straight line) and a three-dimensional object such as a sphere, and instead viewed both as two-dimensional, would this change in perspective allow a straight line to equal a circle? Basically, if I walked from my house to my mailbox, that could be as a hypothetical straight line if viewed two dimensionally not taking in the curvature of the earth. Compare this with a hypothetical walk that I begin at my front door, circumnavigating the world along the equator (Yes, I know my house is not on the equator and walking on water is not possible but go with me here!) and this walk ends at the exact point where I began: my door! Could both of these trips be viewed as straight if I viewed this from a two dimensional perspective? Under these conditions would this perspective then allow a circle to equal a straight line?

309 Days Remain: On patrol in Mosul

Life was more than just getting a killer's information, and then a confession. I was enclosed by our failing war strategy, the austere and isolated environment, and the girlfriend back home. There was also the daily patrol, the driving version of Russian roulette. But over time, I learned how to live in a "middle place," a place between hyper-alert and unconscious. Surprisingly, there is peace in complete submission; knowing that death is so close makes me feel intensely, and intensely living is addictive.

290 Days Remain: Talking with the interpreters in their room

Life comprised a labyrinth of small, dark rooms, where evil men lurked in corners. I wanted to hurt them. But I also hated this power I had over life—it was real and forever. So sometimes I would sit with the interpreters to drink tea, speak Arabic, and discuss Islam. I needed to see their version of the world.

286 Days Remain: My room at the Guest House

On my day off I would escape to my refuge. I would drink little airplane bottles of alcohol and watched chick-flicks. All the love, friends, and sophomoric life difficulties would make me break down. Sometimes, it felt like I watched these movies just so I would feel.

280 Days Remain: The Tigris River seen through razor wire

After a long night of interrogations, I would stand behind thick river reeds beneath a tall eucalyptus tree. Sometimes Saedi would join me. As he silently focused on his smoking, I would listen to the wind in the trees making the branches and leaves speak. During these moments I could escape to natural places beautifully devoid of humans.

259 Days Remain: The 47th Terrorist

Slowly, it became difficult to focus. There was the whimpering and whining and pleading, the repetitions and tangents, the sweet Chai and prayer beads streaming between thumb and forefinger, the ceaseless smoking, and, of course, every habit of every person I lived with. Everything and everyone—including myself—became infuriating.

259 Days Remain: Holding hands with Hashim
My interpreter's daily Arabic classes were serenely rational, and provided deep insight
into Islam. Hashim's was a loving and peaceful God, and I needed this perspective.

252 Days Remain: Saedi and Iraqi guard with a prisoner

One day Saedi crossed my red line. Damn it, I warned him. But if I reported this, he would lose his job, and then where would I be? Our rapport allowed me to prevent real abuse from occurring, and our partnership saved lives.

243 Days Remain: The author jogging at the far end of the Guest House
Sometimes my runs took me to the far end of the base, near the piles of trash and stunted brush, a whole 500 meters away. I no longer cared about the tormenting sniper. I needed the distance.

238 Days Remain: In-processing new prisoners
I could only feel frustration when Amy called and said "I am out of deposit slips" and that she needed me to fix this. She didn't understand the world I lived in, and my distance confused her.

Iraq, 2005

220 Days Remain

I hang up the phone after a call with Amy. I step outside in the early-morning cool to see the sun rise. It's early, but late night her time, and it's October and cold, but even here you can feel the seasons change.

It's so fucking hard between us. I both need her and also feel that this relationship is not right. For me, it's just not working.

I keep telling her how I appreciate all of the things that she does for me but I am confused and I feel desperately alone. I realize I need some "connection," to know that there is someone back home, someone who is thinking of me, someone who cares. This "knowing" somehow makes waking up each morning easier, more bearable. Is this the only reason I continue with her?

Last night was my turn for duty in our communications room, and so this morning I wake up to a stiff back and neck from the cot I slept on. And the conversation I just had with Amy does not help my many pains. After some fresh air, I think that I should write her back, but for some reason I can't write. What should I say? So, instead I watch the sunrise, and I listen to the helicopters buzzing the rooftops and the blaring of Stryker air horns maneuvering. Of course, there is the sound of gunfire and the always-present column of black smoke from some bomb. The last several days have been busy; this is all in preparation for the upcoming referendum. We're trying to keep the terrorists off balance.

Since I had duty last night, today is my day off, but "off" is misleading: if something comes up, if Saedi calls me, if Coalition forces drop by for an unexpected visit, if a bomb goes off, or a mortar hits the base, if a sniper takes a shot, and hopefully misses, or if an Iraqi knocks on the gate to demand compensation for a dead relative, if a terrorist is captured and brought to our cell, if, if, if . . . it seems that something will fucking happen to ensure that this day will not be entirely mine. But if it does happen that today I'm left alone to escape in blissful solitude, and silence, oh blessed silence, then I am planning to spend the day studying Arabic—to wander off into the flow.

I may watch a movie or two. I will certainly jack off. I will drink little airplane bottles of Jack Daniels. I will fall asleep and then I will wake up. There is not much else to do when life is contained within a 100-meter triangle. There is the building where I sleep, the building where Saedi works, and the TOC, our communications room. These three buildings are within a 300-step trip. I may make a diversion once or twice a day: to the Iraqi mess hall, for example, thus changing my existence from a triangle to a square. So, sometimes I decide to spice things up, to put a little adventure in my life. With my bald head exposed to reflecting sunlight, I will take a walk around the perimeter while listening to my iPod, or I will memorize words in Arabic, or I will stand perfectly still and just stare at a pile of burning trash, mesmerized by the winking flames, or search for where the wild things hide, the dogs that whine in the bushes or the feral cats that live under our buildings. On rare occasions I will roam through the several unused buildings looking for rooms I have never explored. And on even rarer occasions, if I am feeling really adventurous, I will go down to the end of the base—a whole 500 meters away—to explore the piles of junk left over from decades of use and then thrown away, all the while daring that fucking sniper to take a shot. If you are looking, here is my middle finger, you asshole!

During these walks, I look up at the green trees or watch the Tigris or stare at a rare cloud float by in an even rarer blue sky. During these walks, it's hard but I try to keep my perspectives distant. When I focus on what is near, on what is close by, I see the trash or dirt or smell the stink. When this happens, I make sure to push my views up and out into the distance, to again focus on the Trees, or the River, or the Horizon. It's amazing how we can choose our perspective and how this small change changes everything.

But then the sound of close or distant gunfire, the blast of a bomb, the rise of black smoke on the horizon, will always pull me back, and then I remember the roaming crosshairs, the guilty or innocent prisoner, or I make sure to stop and talk with an Iraqi guard or a roaming Iraqi soldier. I will say hello and pass the few seconds in polite conversation. We smile and wave and say good-bye and then my walk continues. Always, I will return back to my square and then slowly I fall back into my triangle—my room, the TOC, the interrogation room.

I will go crazy unless I fill each day with something, anything beyond the interrogations. I know that each of us has a very different technique to survive a year of this: prepare a meal in our little kitchen area; watch a stupid movie; read a book or magazine; master the Rubik's Cube; play board games or video games; listen to music; learn Arabic; smoke cigarettes; chew tobacco; exercise; masturbate; or sleep, sleep, sleep. Fuck, I'm so tired of seeing the same nine American faces, hearing the same nine voices, dealing with the same nine personalities day after day after day after day. I am tired of waking up and seeing the same person cooking fucking hamburgers for fucking breakfast, of him leaving our little kitchen smelling of grease in the morning with the pan unclean in the fucking sink. I am tired of the guy who always has a cigarette in his mouth and seeing little wisps of smoke trailing out of his hairy nose as he talks. I am tired of the same person who ceaselessly drinks Mountain Dew and then leaves these cans everywhere. I am tired of drinking disgustingly sweet tea, of dipping flat bread into greasy disgusting soup, of trying to separate the fat from the squares of floating chunks of meatless lamb. I am tired of tobacco-scented air freshener. I am tired of the sniper who can't hit the side of a fucking barn. I am tired of seeing the same terrorists come and go through our prison door and knowing that they have killed and will kill again because they didn't confess, all because I wasn't willing to give in to Saedi's demands, to hurt them in order to get a confession, or maybe some useful information. I am tired of how they all look alike, how they all say the same things. I am tired of hearing them cry and beg for mercy, for forgiveness; well, fuck them. Put a bullet in their head and the world becomes better. I am tired of telling Iraqis to not abuse the bomber, the rapist, the American soldier-killer; this abuse is what keeps them in jail, and maybe, just maybe, keeps them from ever killing again.

I am tired of wondering how long this all can last because it's not just one thing or several things, it's the accumulation of everything and the cumulative effect of a thousand things. The hundreds of patrols and close calls and waking up to think and hope that maybe today will be my last, and the peace this thought brings me, the fucking peace it brings me.

Shit, I am just tired of fucking everything. I want to close my eyes and sleep, to sleep for a year, maybe more, and then to wake up to friends and family and smiles and love, all of the good that I know must still be out there somewhere. But, as if miraculously, the day comes to an end. I climb into bed. I watch a stupid movie, which makes me . . . well, cry, because it's addictive to feel something, and something helps me sleep, and going to sleep is committing to another day in this place.

I rest my head on the pillow.

I take a deep breath.

I close my eyes.

Then I wake up, sometimes fresh, often not, to reenter the surreal cycle I am increasingly unable to navigate and the ongoing seemingly endless interrogations and conversations with Saedi. Unless by some fluke my sniper actually hits his target, I will continue day after day by telling myself: "Just breathe. Just breathe. Think on all the reasons you want to go home—soon, sooner than you think, this place will become no more than a memory."

⌁

I open my eyes—another day.

I stay in bed and prepare.

Ramadan is in full swing, which means that the pace of events has drastically slowed—so I spend a few hours studying Arabic and drinking coffee. I get a call from a now-awake Saedi. After pleasantries and one interrogation, I drive the short distance across town to attend an Iraqi Army meeting. We're preparing for the upcoming constitution referendum.

We drive as fast as a 10,000-pound armored HUMVEE can go. The crowds and traffic we drive through make today's drive difficult, and this patrol should be terrifying, but it's not. I enjoy being in the turret when we're out on patrol. It's relaxing.

We all have high hopes that things will soon get better with the referendum and the new constitution. The Iraqis I speak with believe it will. I hope that the Iraqi citizens will take responsibility for their own fucking lives so I can go home, but I don't hold my breath—it seems they've learned helplessness. It will take a new generation to grow up in a secure environment for things to really change. But I still hope.

⌁

"I am angry," says Saedi, "Mr. Bill. All of us are."

I'm so glad I came over to say hello, because today's discussion has turned to the Iraqi legal system, which is, well, a fucking disaster. I'm tired of having to deal with it, how the terrorist is caught and then, for some reason, somewhere, the terrorist is released back on the streets to kill again . . . released by the interrogator, because if the insurgent does not confess there will be no trial; by the policeman who takes a bribe; by the judge who is scared for his life or his family or who is appointed because he is weak. Or perhaps it is the lawyer who works for the terrorists; by the main Baghdad jail because a political party demanded release; by the powerful relative who calls the governor or police chief. Maybe in a week, or at most several months, the terrorist will eventually come back . . . and all citizens know this. So why should the citizen care? I cannot get angry at them for not working to stop terrorists. Would I work to stop the terrorist if my family and I lived here? I would hope so, but I just don't know. I don't want to try to understand this doubt, because it's easier when I just wanted to kill the insurgent. The months of interrogating have caused this inner conflict: why have I started to care more about why they fight, and less about how to get their confession?

"This is important for Americans," continues Saedi's angry tirade. "Now there is a belief by many Iraqi citizens—this is even believed by the Iraqi Army and police, and even I believe it—that Americans really do not want to stop terrorism within Iraq."

I can only nod and empathize and give noncommittal grunts.

We catch killers, we interrogate them for a few days, and if we have enough information, mostly which depends on a confession, we turn them over to the Iraqi police. Then they enter the "system." If there is no confession or overwhelming evidence—an impossible thing in a counterinsurgency—they are then released back to the streets, to kill again. Some prisoners that Saedi and I release even end up right back here, in our jail, to start the cycle all over again. It's all fucking bullshit.

And because of this, I know the single most important topic that now consumes almost every minute of every big meeting I have with Iraqis is the lack of strong procedures necessary to convict, imprison, and punish terrorists. And by "strong procedures," they also mean the latitude to use hard interrogation methods, for me to stop staying "no," because from their perspective this inability—my rules, my boundaries—means an insurgent will quickly return to the street and neighborhood with little to no punishment. The longer I am here, the more I realize this disease infects us all. When terrorists are released, it causes anger, fear, and complacency within the populace, which then allows the insurgency to grow. This insurgency is a never-ending cycle; it's beyond frustrating; these killers are literally always within arm's reach and there is nothing I can fucking do!

We get up from our "talk," and we go sit in a big room, which we use for large meetings. Today, Saedi and I are speaking with various Iraqi government officials from across Mosul. To my left is Saedi. To his left is the deputy police chief. Then there are two employees from the Ministry of Interior unit who live right across the river from us. There are two officers from another Iraqi Army unit who work on the other side of town. There is a neighborhood Muktar and the director of the city's Incident Response Unit. There is an employee from the Office of the Mayor. Today, there are a lot of Iraqis sitting here, and their anger is focused on me.

"What are human rights with terrorists?" the Muktar begins. "If someone kills my brother, I cannot testify against him, because I know that soon he will be released and then *I* will be killed." I am getting overwhelmed with their frustration and hopelessness. I am seeing that most interrogators now wear masks because they know that the chances are good that the person they talk with will be back on the streets and will look for them and their family.

"Sending terrorists to Abu Ghraib for six months? This only means they organize some other group," the deputy police chief tells me. "Many believe that Abu Ghraib is only gathering terrorists and allowing them to meet. It is a place for an Iraq-wide terrorist conference," he continues.

I nod because I know that this same frustration affects the informant, the police officer, the lawyer, and the judge. It seems that no Iraqi remains unaffected. It even frustrates me, the American, to no end.

The Iraqi police officer then decides to speak up. "We need strong procedures so you can divide between the citizens that are good and bad. With a terrorist leader, you must be tough and do your best to confront him with harsh punishment so his members stop fighting. Till now, there are no procedures that do this."

I just nod.

"People are upset," says the man from the Ministry of Interior. "They do not want to give information about terrorists. They say 'Okay, I will give you information; but will you stop him?' My answer to these citizens can only be: 'I will detain him.' I cannot honestly say more, because I would be lying; several of Saedi's informants have been killed. This is a horrible situation. Judges are either scared for their family or their own lives, or they support the terrorists. Judges delay a case for a while. Then a month or so later, the terrorist goes before the judge and the judge asks 'Are you a terrorist?' 'No,' says the terrorist. The judge will say 'Then why did you confess?' 'Because they tortured me,' says the terrorist. 'Where is the citizen then who accuses this man?' says the judge. Of course everyone knows that the Iraqi who tells on his neighbors cannot testify! So the judge just releases the terrorist."

God, this is frustrating, because I now see that even when a confession is forced, this confession will likely make no difference. If they are always just released, is killing a terrorist the only way to stop them? I have been here more than six months and I am disturbed at these thoughts and bothered by my inability to give good answers to Iraqis who are mad at me. And I feel morally obliged to have answers: America is the cause of this mess that now only Iraqis can clean up.

"Whenever you create a government," the deputy police chief continues, "there are always two sides of interest, and now there is a problem. They want the Sunnis to be involved with the election and participate in the government and they did. The chief of the Sunni Coalition has said 'There are six thousand Sunnis in jail, and when they are released I will participate.' And so if the government says tomorrow that strong procedures will be established, that these Sunnis will not be released, this Sunni leader will not accept this and the problems will not be solved. But things will only get harder, not easier, and now is the time to establish strict procedures to fight terrorism."

I nod.

"Strong procedures prevent terrorism," the employee from the Mayor's Office tells me. "This is hurting Americans as much as us, because it affects your politics. It affects your policy of democracy for the Middle East, so it is more of a problem for you than for us."

I nod.

"If I was the U.S. leader in this area," says the employee of the mayor, "I would sit with the police chief and the governor and press them to go to Baghdad and to assign a strong judge with strong rules. This is the most important. This is more important than the Iraqi Army or Iraqi police or catching terrorists. We need someone to listen to our problems, because we know what is going on with the citizens."

I nod. But really I am frustrated, with the terrorist and with the Iraqi. Every Iraqi has a solution, but they are never willing to solve it themselves. It is always someone else who is responsible.

Almost every meeting I have with Iraqis moves onto this topic and their frustrations; they blame me, the face of America, for America removed the only government that provided security, and America is the power behind the new government and therefore also behind the Iraqi policies and procedures which are the result of American pressures and demands—or a lack of them.

Our meeting ends without any resolution; they always end this way. These meetings are only an opportunity for everyone to vent, more often than not at me. So, after the meeting Saedi and I move back to talk in his office.

"This is bad for Americans," he says after our small talk and first cup of chai. "Because of your actions, even your friends are upset. Many times I talk with people and ask for their help and they say, 'No, I will not cooperate with Americans.' For the American war against terrorism, if they cannot even get their friends to trust them, how are they going to get the citizen's trust? I trust you. I know you are not cheating us, but there are some American procedures which make you seem dishonest and hurt the citizen more than help. For instance, I understand your rules and laws. But for most citizens who are uneducated, they do not understand you. They cannot know that when Americans say 'human rights' or when you release prisoners, it is because of your laws and procedures and rules of evidence. But the citizen says 'See, the Americans released the terrorist. They do not want them to go away. They do not want to really stop terrorism.'"

America is the "face" on this counterinsurgency, and I am the focus of the citizens' blame. What Saedi describes is pervasive and easy to hide from those who stand on the outside looking in. Is this view true, this belief they have? The truth or falseness of Iraqi perceptions is irrelevant. Perceptions and misperceptions are powerful and have an impact. They affect how people think and act, and our mission relies on perceptions to fight the insurgent.

"There is another rumor," Saedi tells me. "It says that America itself is emplacing IEDs. This rumor is believed because the Americans have not worked to have strong procedures. People say 'Under Saddam I only got ten dollars and I was poor, but at least I felt safe.' They say 'Fuck all the money if it is not safe.'"

This situation frustrates and disillusions Iraqis. From the perspective I am afforded, from the chair I sit on in this room, from the cell where I interrogate, or from the office where I talk with informants, I see that the continuous release of prisoners distorts the true number of terrorists that are really present in this society. Citizens think that there must be thousands, when in fact there are only hundreds, and there is nothing I can do.

"First, kill the terrorist," continues Saedi, "or at least ensure that we keep the terrorists in jail. Iraqi citizens will then believe that terrorists will be stopped, they will then help stop terrorists and terrorists will be scared and stop. But because there are no strong procedures, we are confused. I am only one intelligence officer, but you and I have captured over one hundred terrorists already. And this has not affected the situation. You know this, Mr. Bill. And that is just us, and a portion of Mosul! Imagine how many people have been captured by all the forces in Mosul, the Iraq Army, the police, the Americans, the Ministry of Interior. Who is the terrorist and who isn't? They come and go, in and out of jail so fast they seem like tens of thousands and even more."

I am tired, so I decide to play with my cell-phone ringer. I pretend I am getting a phone call. I stand up and start to leave.

"Wait, Mr. Bill. America does not understand! Remember the neighborhood of al-Sukar and how you gave candy to those two girls, and they refused? This is what the children were thinking," says Saedi: "'If you do not do anything for me, why are you giving me that chocolate?'"

"I know," I respond as I drag myself out the office door; and on the way back to my room, I can't stop thinking about those two girls who smiled but refused my candy. Why doesn't the world respond the way it's supposed to? Because I see everything and everyone through the filter of my own culture, my own experience. My wants are unrealistic and my perceptions are untrue. The longer I'm here, and the more I learn, the more uncertain and conflicted I become about everyone's assumed guilt.

Germany, September 2011

16 Days Remain

I will forget about the mathematician and just ask myself: What if I changed my perspective so that both the circle and the line are viewed in three dimensions (or more)? Well, aren't they? In my previous perspective, I was comparing apples and oranges. A straight line exists in reality, and reality is not two-dimensional (is it?). Instead, in this reality a "straight" line does in fact have a curve.

So, if I were to pull this line out to a distance of infinity minus one, would not the ends eventually meet, somewhere and sometime in the future? And is this then not the same thing as a circle? Yes, I now see it's true, the differences we see so clearly are in truth the misjudged attributes of the very same thing, which makes absolute sense—opposites are only an illusion, opposites are really the same thing, and this is eye-opening. But then the insane can use logic to convince the crazy of anything. . . .

ts to catch. The war will always be here waiting for
to catch up. So sit with me and have some tea." So what
n when we leave and take our hand off the pressure-
at we've set to high? How long till we see the results?
at is my thinking—Iraqis, and Saedi, take a generational
He doesn't define time as one-year military deployments
year terms of office. But he does believe that it is a race
the U.S. and the insurgency: Can a stable democracy be
the security force be trained, and the counterinsurgency
se its "American face," before the insurgency organizes?
an immense responsibility for anyone, but especially for
who seems to shoulder this responsibility as his own.

ckily, the average Iraqi soldier rarely focuses on this para-
larger picture. Instead, they focus on the micro problems;
on in a terrorist cell, several terrorists in a few houses, and at
a cell in a neighborhood. It seems that this is a good approach
ounterinsurgency, where the cumulative effect of a thousand
pendent counterinsurgent actions is greater than the sum of
parts. Americans could take a lesson from this.

Here at the Guest House, our actions are only a tiny part of this
seen and unintended macro strategy. Here, our task is to just
pture or kill insurgents in a small portion of this very large city.
ere, life is a repeating cycle of intelligence collection, insurgent
apture, and the subsequent interrogation and exploitation of our
aptured insurgents, which then leads to the capture of more insurgents who we then interrogate in order to capture more. There is not
a well-defined start or end point to this very unique Iraqi targeting
cycle; it continues until actionable information is unavailable.
But this cycle seems to never end because there is always a new
prisoner to start the cycle again. America is no different, we're just
more, and much more technologically capable—we're a capability
in search of a requirement. And the more proficient we become,
the more threats we seem to find, and even if we were to capture
or kill them all, our measure of who is a "terrorist" just lowers,

Iraq, 2005

204 Days Remain

The nights are getting longer, and I'm using this extra time to
understand the why of everything: Why do Iraq citizens become
insurgents? Why do these people fight themselves, and us? What
are their motivations, and why do they kill? And why do I seem
to care about understanding? But what I'm learning about the
individual is no less distressing than learning about the interrogation. Getting killers to talk is easy compared with this, this need
to understand what it is we are fighting.

Today, I sit on my rooftop; I take a step back from the killer's
face, to instead gaze out on an entire city. As I look out over the
hundreds of thousands who live under tens of thousands of rooftops, I begin to see a pattern in the disorder form: it's this chaos
that prevents the insurgency from winning, from achieving its
larger, "strategic" goals. But it's also this same chaos that allows
the violence to continue without end. Is this the absurdity that
causes so much heartache?

. . . I hear a Styker air horn; I focus in on this patrol as it winds
down a nearby street. Cars part to make way, then I hear some

gunshots from the north; I swivel my head to the left to see black smoke, a few columns, on the horizon. There's a large explosion to the west; two Kiowa helicopters fly by. . . .

We are in a dew-loop, unable to break out of the insurgent/counterinsurgent kill-and-so-kill-and-so-kill cycle. The insurgency can't win, but neither can America, and so the killing just keeps on going, keeps repeating. To what end? Who is the enemy that we are really fighting? Is the enemy even a person? Or do we mindlessly flail at symptoms, while not even understanding the sickness?

These interrogations have pried my eyes open, and what I see is both mystifying and terrifying.

Because this insurgency is unified by its hatred of the unbearable-but-necessary American "occupation"; and to a lesser degree, it is justified by Islam. It is motivated by base, selfish greed, sustained by a complacent and passive citizenry, fed by a nascent and untrained security force and an unstable environment. It is fueled by bad American policies and counterproductive military tactics and constrained by limited resources and competing interests. These characteristics are difficult for the Iraqis, and for the Americans, to comprehend, let alone overcome. Yet this still does not come close to describing the true complexity of what we fight, and of what I interrogate. One Iraqi told me: "How to solve this is sometimes too much. I am now seeing the only thing that Saddam Hussein was good for . . . making sure Iraqis don't fight each other. You caused this, and you now occupy my country."

And then there is one small consequence of this fucked-up situation which has become personal.

Saedi is overwhelmed.

He takes the job of fighting the insurgency as his responsibility, and he's overcome by this adventure to create a democracy in a nation surrounded by dictators and theocracies. But Saedi tries to make a difference one insurgent at a time. But the insurgency is skilled at shaping local and international opinions and perceptions:

terrorists hand-carry the v[...]
national media in Baghdad, [...]
media, those violence-addict[...]
from a distance, looking for [...]
in to deliver the mayhem to th[...]
then to a world that craves vi[...]
audience creates the story; and th[...]
personal reward. Fuck it to no er[...]
talks to vent. It must be the stress [...]
it sure is driving me crazy!

I do, however, appreciate the ch[...]
that America is the "glue" that bin[...]
as long as Americans are here the te[...]
fighting is strengthened; no matter h[...]
other, they hate Americans more. Con[...]
the referendum will be a success and the [...]
buckle under the pressure of sensitive pul[...]
a result the U.S. military will respond to u[...]
scale back or withdraw. Add to this his bel[...]
military is essential to the country's survival [...]
is formed and the Iraqi security forces are tr[...]
eral recently told me that Iraq is now a nation[...]
competes to advance a thousand different ver[...]
And I agree, yet at the same time we are moral[...]
righting the boat we've capsized.

In Mosul there are Arab, Persian, Turkmer[...]
agents, American soldiers and diplomats, idealisti[...]
civilians, international businessmen and criminals, i[...]
ists, and the vulture media. Iraqis must contend wit[...]
the insurgency uses it to their advantage. Though he[...]
it in these same words, Saedi knows that the insurge[...]
perceived as a struggle for liberation and so only cont[...]
possible. This morning, Saedi told me: "American so[...]
always in a rush and working all the time and there wi[...]

leading to more "terrorists" to capture and interrogate. And then there will come a time when the National Mission Force goes on raids to capture goat herder Abu: "he did sympathize with the terrorists! He's a high value individual!"

It's only natural, it's organizational survival, but fuck, it feels like I'm living a sick and twisted version of Groundhog Day. It is both fascinating to watch and disturbing to experience, this view of myself through the prism of a foreign prison. But still I try to make sense of things, of everything.

As an Iraqi intelligence officer, Saedi holds a unique and very powerful position, one that engenders both fear and respect. These are two emotions that he leverages to keep the "terrorists" confessing. He is thus able to operate with greater autonomy than most other Iraqi Army officers. It seems that the process of targeting the insurgency and capturing insurgents begins and ends with him.

There are glaring limitations to this: a reliance on targeting the insurgent versus solving underlying social, economic, and political problems; a lack of information-collection technology and, therefore, a dependence solely on the human to provide information; a cultural and organizational aversion to cooperating with or sharing intelligence; no organizational systems, standards, or individual desire to amass data on an insurgent or on an insurgent group; and an ever-present preference for speed over thoroughness. Despite—and in some instances, because of—these limitations, Saedi is good at what he does: finding, capturing, and interrogating insurgents.

Unlike in the U.S. military, Saedi fills the role that numerous Americans hold. He runs source networks and gathers the information on an insurgent or insurgent group. He oversees and conducts the interrogations and exploits the detainee. He is also the one who has the authority to conduct an operation to capture or kill a person. And sometimes we go out on these missions ourselves. These characteristics are more personal and cultural than organizational; but regardless, it is fucking effective and I'm both lucky and cursed to be immersed in it, to get this different perspective.

U.S. soldiers around Mosul always comment that the Iraqi military organizational culture lacks systems and procedures. But I am starting to see that, at least here in Mosul, this lack of "organization culture" may be an advantage, and may be a trait we should try to emulate.

In the U.S. military, the many soldiers who conduct source operations, analyze the information, prepare the target packages, action the information, and lastly conduct the interrogations and then disseminate the information are often separated by time, distance, and—most importantly—organizational culture. This causes lapses both in time and purpose. Another factor that cannot be understated is that the U.S. military focuses on procedures and time schedules. Saedi is always bitching about how we are "always having meetings and then more meetings again and then we talk about attacking a house and capturing an insurgent for weeks sometimes! This is so frustrating."

One of the problems is that Americans conceptualize the counterinsurgency in terms of daily, weekly, biweekly, and monthly "rhythms," where there are schedules to follow, where schedules have briefings, and authorizations, etc., and that these gates must be passed through before actions can be authorized and anything can happen. Americans don't like to admit it, and mostly we are very unaware of it, but following a process consumes our attention and at times constrains our effectiveness. Also, the "process" is why this fighting, the killing, has become a perpetual thing. It's a man-made "system" that becomes animated, it takes on a life of its own, independent of but dependent on the people who run it and feed it. It's amazing, but I now realize that war can become a learned trait, just a habit that you instinctually keep performing: war is like breathing.

This very American trait, of being one part of a massive warring organism that instinctually flails against a foe it does not understand, is far removed from my life here at the Guest House. Here the cultural chasm is not as wide between those conducting the counterinsurgency and those persons fighting in the insurgency. But this chasm is especially deep and wide between the American military and the Iraqi insurgent. Though it is certainly the American government and the American military's intent to "win," sometimes it seems that our policies, our strategies, and especially our tactics have an unintended and opposite effect. We are not learning from our mistakes, mistakes that just make the insurgency stronger. We're losing this war, and I'm watching it fucking happening.

We live behind the walls of secure American bases, our vacuum-sealed, delusional, and self-imposed bubbles, and we're scared to get out and walk, to come out from behind the safety of our razor wire, armored vehicles, and smothering protective gear. We're scared to interact with the citizen, to learn that they need protecting more than the insurgent needs killing. We don't respect those we are sworn to protect and so we just fight and fight, relying solely on our military might, measuring success by easily quantifiable first-order effects. Yes, we're good at killing insurgents, but we're blind to how this killing affects the citizen.

Can we learn that killing the insurgent is an insufficient and less important detail? Some part of me thinks it's not possible for Americans to think in a different way; it's easier this way, to always lumber forward then it is to mentally change course. So instead we'll just continue our fighting, and American soldiers and Iraqi civilians will continue their dying.

Iraq, 2005

198 Days Remain

It's mid-day and I'm tired—learning Arabic isn't appealing to me right now—so I e-mail Amy and thank her for the Halloween gift box she sent. She sent me a wig for Halloween.

The idea of celebrating Halloween in this place is fucking ridiculous, but when I put on the mullet wig, the Iraqis are amused. Amy seemed to be in a good mood in her last letter, but she says there's something she wants to talk about. What now? She doesn't say, but then today she's upset that I don't call much. I know I could call and I tell myself that I should call, that I will, but then something always happens. Calling is not that convenient, it costs a lot, plus I know there are Americans listening in on my conversation. But frankly, I just don't want to talk to her much anymore. Our conversations are a world apart, and static slurs the words; the connection is slipping.

What can I talk about: Interrogations? Bombs? Mortar rounds? Sniper fire? Dead bodies? Saedi's insistence? My growing doubt about every prisoner's guilt or my supposed virtue? Should we talk about how when I drive and the traffic starts to crush in on every side, the hairs on my arms start to rise, and my boss freezes glassy-eyed? How he's scared and unable to make a decision, to provide any leadership, unable to tell us what he wants us to do? Do I talk about how when this happens, which is more and more lately, I have to just take charge? Do I tell her how fear is starting to paralyze him and many of us, and how I worry that death will be the consequence? I don't, because I know that she will not understand. This reality will just bother her and make her more worried. My reality will only disturb her. So instead we talk about chores, finances, and her dinner at a restaurant; I like to hear of these things, but they also seem so inconsequential, so insignificant. We are each out of touch with the other's reality.

I am starting to feel we are not right for each other and that this deployment has provided me some distance to see our relationship objectively. But at the same time, living here makes me need her all the more. It's depressing, and fucking hypocritical; so when I end my talk with Amy, I go sit down with three of our informants. I decide to start training them on the use of a GPS; perhaps this distraction will keep my mind off Amy.

The first step is to teach them how to turn the device on and mark their position. Teaching Iraqis is frustrating. I struggle with this for an hour and barely get past the "turning on" button, so I decide to give up for the day and focus instead on putting some target packages together with Saedi. For Americans, this process of targeting the terrorist is deliberate. For Iraqis, capturing or killing an insurgent is very fluid, and hasty.

When it comes to intelligence, Saedi always seems to desire speed, as opposed to thoroughness. In most cases, a single report of a terrorist and a person's willingness to guide him to the house is all that is needed to take action. Once we get to the house, the Iraqis will capture every male who is of "terrorist age" and will question the females on site but not detain them. The whole matter of who the "real" terrorist is comes later, as part of the interrogation. Saedi's, and my experience, is that if one man in the house is accused of terrorism, then the chances are that most of those in the house either support him or at least have credible information about him. Culpable or not, everyone has some information which will somehow help us determine who the "real" terrorist is. Interrogate them all, gather up all this information, and we usually can get someone to confess. Saedi then uses the interrogation process as a means of amassing the intelligence that we were not able to attain from the informants in the first place.

The U.S. military's tendency, however, is almost the exact opposite. With our technology and our many means of gathering information about a single terrorist, we first focus on amassing data. This data then eventually leads an analyst to a conclusion that someone is a person worthy of dedicating limited resources against. They put together a target package, and this package allows a leader to insert and prioritize a mission into a unit's targeting cycle. Eventually, this will lead to a raid sometime in the near future; within the next week, or two, or more. And then when the mission does occur, the actual killing of a terrorist is viewed as the conclusion of this cycle. We overlook that each terrorist or small group of terrorists does not operate in a vacuum. Our technological superiority allows us to diminish the importance of the human, and isolates us from the people, a tragic thing when a successful counterinsurgency depends almost solely on the human factor.

Within a neighborhood, a city, a province, and a country, insurgents are interconnected by a spiderweb of direct and indirect lines; the capture of one is not an end in itself, but is a means to find more. This is one of the principal differences between the U.S. and Iraqi military culture. But these traits are both good and bad, because in many instances, this will cause Saedi to be myopic—to not see the "larger picture"—how each prisoner is just one small part of a larger tapestry, not just information in a vacuum.

And Saedi loves information. These prisoners are analogous to American technology; to Saedi, each prisoner is a new airplane, satellite, or unmanned drone, and each provides new and more information that he hungers for. Each prisoner he catches and interrogates is an emotional culmination point—that is, until he captures someone different, interrogates them, and sees that this new interrogation will lead to *more* "terrorists" that he can capture and interrogate.

And then there is me, the fly on the wall who wearies of this never-ending cycle. Because regardless of each "killer's" guilt, and of my hate, I still feel each prisoner's fear and pain. And I'm drained, unable to walk away, to disengage.

~

We have been in communications blackout for the last two days. I tell Amy that this is why I can't write, but she doesn't believe me. She swears there is another girl in competition. I just swear.

A communications blackout occurs when a U.S. soldier in Mosul is killed. When this happens, and it happens a lot now, they shut down all Internet and phone access for the American military. This way, the military is able to notify the family before the news gets out over e-mail. It is very sad, and when they do a blackout it is almost like an unintentional moment of silence is pulled down over the city. The soldier's access to the Internet is like the grease that keeps the war machine humming along, a hearty dose of morale for all; so when a blackout happens, it's as if we are forced to acknowledge what we desperately, unconsciously deny: war is sobering, there are real-life consequences: American sons and daughters are dying.

It has been raining all day, and it is really a refreshing change. To see clouds and the wind, which makes everything smell fresh and clean. The ground is wet and the air is cold. A fresh rain brings a whole new feeling to the place. It is supposed to rain tomorrow too, and I am looking forward to this.

I have been using my iPod a lot. I download music I borrowed from another soldier, and I spent a few hours today organizing my music. It seems a waste of time, but I have to find something, day in and day out, to make the time pass. Here, time is no longer alive. Time is like a thick fog that hangs over a river. Living here is like taking a never-ending walk in this foggy soup—time seems to slow and the clarity of events blur. And I walk forever and quickly get nowhere; as I move, the shapes just pass around me, through me, over and over, and still I never arrive anywhere.

Living here is like this, and I have to find things to do, to fill those 1,440 minutes, those 86,400 seconds of every day that I never noticed before. There are 31,536,000 seconds in the year, until the day I return home, and 31,536,000 seconds is a lot of time; so what do I do besides interrogate killers, survive the patrol and the girlfriend back home, and watch us lose this war?

I go to meetings with Saedi and my interpreters, study Arabic, organize my music, work out, run, watch a movie, speak Arabic with soldiers, make breakfast, lunch, and dinner, sit on my rooftop and dip tobacco. I am even thinking about learning to play the guitar. Yesterday I had another close call. We were attending a large meeting and mortars began to fall—just another event to pass the time, in this case the time it took for the bombs to fall and for everyone to run and hide. That was 46 seconds: 0.00014586504312531 percent of this year.

Germany, September 2011

12 Days Remain

4:07 P.M.

"What is real and what is a dream?" I scream. I don't know if these flashbacks and thoughts will ever stop; but like any natural thing, I hope for some kind of equilibrium. . . . Close your eyes. Breathe deep. Breathe hard. . . . Does everything have a perfect opposite? I think so. But do we perfectly partner with our opposite to find happiness? Or is everything and does everyone just search for a perfect complement, that "thing" that is necessary for extremes to balance? Is this "realizing our potential"? But what if complements can't talk?

4:11 P.M.

What if the differences that are so necessary are the same differences that push us apart?
Searching, listening, interpreting.
Not understanding. Judging.
Imperfect people

Needing unconditional love
Are they destined for unhappiness?

4:12 P.M.
Since we all interact with the world
By interpreting external stimuli
If something is frustrating
I see two choices:
Learn the language,
Or depart.
Is all unhappiness
Our unique ways of
Acting out our frustrations?
Is life just us not getting our way?

Iraq, 2005

191 Days Remain

Today began by sitting down with Mohammed, the young son of Maher, my Arab interpreter. Mohammed lives at home with his mom, but he loves to come to our base to spend the day with his father. I like spending time with him—he reminds me of the children in Iraq. They do not yet have the hatreds, the animosities, the intolerance, or the distrust that is present in almost every adult. But the kids are different.

During last night's interrogations, we had children present; Saedi and I were comparing notes, and in the corner of the office were a few of our prisoners' kids. We brought them and their mom in to use in the interrogation of their father. They now wait in the corner of our office, but they move closer at my invitation. I hand each a crayon and paper, and they hide their joy well; it's sad to think that the crayons I hand over are probably the first they have ever received.

I'm especially taken with this little boy and girl who look about three and six. They are skinny and so tiny, but they seem so much older. Here, young kids seem older than they really are, and I sense this untimely experience in this little boy and girl's body language and facial expressions.

A few hours later, we allow them to leave, so I take them outside to stand near our vehicles while they wait for their ride back home. Before they leave, I give them a beanie baby, but still they just stand and stare. I know they are scarred—and scared—and that I've only made it worse: I have their father in prison. But I tell myself that this is a good thing and that now their lives will be better, even if they don't yet know it. My convincing doesn't make me feel better.

~

The room is full: maybe fifty or so Iraqis, and all are eating. I look around and think that the Iraqi chow hall really isn't such a bad place. There are four rows of long tables, and each can seat about eight people. Over each table are white and black spotted chandeliers, which other people call a long curly-cue sticky flytrap. But I pretend that they are chandeliers—glass chandeliers, in fact.

Today, there are six other Iraqis sitting next to me, but we do not talk. In Kurdish culture, you don't socialize when you eat, so I just hover over a bowl of greasy lamb soup that is mostly grease and little lamb. To my front, in the center of the table, are communal dishes of surprisingly fresh vegetables: cucumbers, tomatoes, and bell peppers. They really are nice looking vegetables, but unfortunately I don't like cucumbers, tomatoes, or bell peppers; I may have to change that.

But thank God! To my front I see Laughing Cow cheese!

I love these little circles of happy cow cheese; the little tiny circles of processed cheese that are enclosed in foil and have a little sticker of a cheesy smiling cow on the front foil wrapper. I love these little circles of truly bad cheese, and it is hard to find the words to describe how much I love them. Also, thank God, I see piles of warm flat bread! I love these little circles of flat bread.

I don't care if they roll the dough on the concrete floors with unwashed hands. I love these circles of flat bread. I reach over my bowl of grease, ignore the vegetables, and grab a couple of smiling cows and one warm piece of speckled bread. And I spread and I spread and I eat. Ah . . . like manna from Heaven. I smile. Flat bread spread with Laughing Cow is my bliss, my safety net. It's amazing how such an insignificant thing can bring such a big smile, so I chomp in pleasure and use this quiet time of eating with fifty Iraqis to think.

I am beginning to understand how these terrorists not only survive but thrive, how they live in, operate within, and take sanctuary from the population of Mosul. Monthly, dozens of informants tell Saedi and me that some insurgent is a husband, a son, a daughter, an in-law, a friend, or a father. That the killer "lives in our home," "he lives next door," "he rents an apartment above me," or "I see them come and go in a house around the corner," "my Imam supports them," "they have meetings at this mosque," "I saw a car with three armed men and I saw them kidnap a young girl," "I saw men kill a policeman," or "I saw some men plant a bomb."

I hear these statements over and over again, and after six months of this I'm starting to get a sense of who the killer is, and what motivates him to fight: anger, religion, fear, power, greed, and prestige. I am starting to see that these motivations are only the first layer. If you peel the onion skin back, you see the corrupt, inept, or complacent government leaders, employees, and businessmen; ineffective security forces; overseas spiritual approval and guidance; foreign money; negative media greedily fanning hatred's flames; foreign intelligence services; and then, the all-important, critical ingredient that creates the citizen's passivity—our own policies, strategies, and heavy-handed tactics. Oh, there is also "al-Qaeda," but for most insurgents this is a self-prescribed ideological label to justify a thousand and one selfish actions. "AQ" lets evil people realize their true potential.

These and countless more factors merge to create the conditions that are necessary for the insurgency to prosper, which allows the terrorist to plant the IED that will go off on the side of my vehicle. The end effect, the killer planting the bomb, is what everyone seems to focus on, the obvious but less important thing. No one seems to care about the motivation or how to counter it. What I now realize is that for this one very obvious action, there are countless more steps that are rarely seen but are as much—if not more—important to understand. I'm starting to think of these as "enablers," the conditions that allow the insurgent to detonate the bomb or to cut off the head or to shoot the gun.

Yesterday morning, I was on patrol and crossing the Tigris. The sun was rising, and for some reason I began to imagine: If I were to hypothetically stand next to the insurgent at that very last moment before he plants the bomb that goes "boom" and if I were to reel the tape in reverse, what would I see? I would see the citizen who watches us from a rooftop, from the window. I would see the car that is filled with explosives, and then all the people who saw us put it there. I would see our house and the other residents who know who we are, the neighbors, and the nosy kid across the street who is always watching. I would see our cache that sits in an empty field in the middle of a neighborhood surrounded by watching windows. I would see the numerous people we interact with to purchase and then make the bomb . . . there are just so many steps, so many people, who witness our seemingly simple act of blowing up a bomb to kill an American. And I realize that we do not live, or operate, in a vacuum, and at any time any one of these countless people could have done something, anything, to stop me. It would be so easy. So why don't they? Why do so many look away from the killing?

"Mr. Bill," says a jundee, disturbing my flatbread with Laughing Cow mental orgasm. "New prisoners just arrived. Saedi would like to speak with you. He is in his office."

Germany, September 2011

12 Days Remain

4:15 P.M.

I feel something.

Question: Does the interaction of imperfect complex systems create an imperfect universe?

Question: What is the result of the interaction of numerous imperfect complex systems?

Question: Is there a process that I can't see taking place?

Question: We can see patterns in the chaos; but is knowing and measuring these patterns possible? Or must we just have faith?

Question: Are we neither opposites nor complements? Are we differences that need each other to reach our full potential?

Question: Are we subatomic elements on a bigger scale?

Tangent: That is an interesting first question to run toward a logical conclusion.

Question to the Wind: God, what is happiness? Is it unconditional love striving to hear a truth?

Stop . . . stop . . . stop this. I have to stop, to control my mind because too many things are happening, too many things are going wrong. I'm scared. I'm covered in itchy scabs, and I must scratch—I can't help it—which only restarts the bleeding. Even now, this very afternoon, as I wait on this train platform on my way home from work, the ceaseless thinking takes over.

I have to tell someone about this. I have to. If not for me, then for my family; because lately, I've started to imagine doing something really, really stupid . . . I am blissfully smiling. I imagine myself taking a step . . . and floating.

Iraq, 2005

180 Days Remain

Six prisoners have disappeared. I don't know what to do.

No Iraqi tells me; I'm just doing some checking, and unexpectedly I find out that they are gone. No one seems to know where. Gone where?

I immediately speak with Saedi and ask where these prisoners went. He tells me that he doesn't know, and I believe him.

Because these weren't his prisoners. They were prisoners in another Iraqi prison that I'm remotely responsible for. But I still demand that he find out.

I have never made such a forceful and immediate demand of Saedi.

I don't command Saedi. I advise. So, he's pissed about this "order," but he's more pissed that I've chosen to not look away, because looking away would be easy, and now not averting my eyes will cause problems. So I know this will have consequences on our relationship.

But fuck! I have to do something.

So I tell my boss that prisoners are missing, and then spend the rest of the day looking into what actually happened.

That was two days ago, and what I eventually found out is that these prisoners were driven north into Kurdistan. Fuck. I am pissed, and I demand that Saedi use his connections to bring these prisoners back to Mosul. I tell him to find a way to bring these men back to our prison. "Saedi, I want them back here, in our prison. I want to see them. Now!"

Well, this afternoon, some Iraqi soldiers stopped by to drop off these missing prisoners.

We line them up along the outside wall to do a quick count and when they bring them in and hand them over, I do my usual thing: I strip each one, take pictures from every possible angle. I need to document the condition they came to me in. This way, I can prove if any abuse occurs while they are in our prison.

The problem with this is that insurgents lead hard lives, and when they get caught they often look like they've been tortured. Usually I won't be able to tell; but if the abuse is from an Iraqi soldier's hands, then hopefully the preponderance of visible evidence looks recent. This way I get a hunch. So I take my pictures; this time it's different—there are lashes, bruising, and cuts all over. This time, I know that these prisoners were horribly tortured. Today the abuse is obvious.

Do I report this to American authorities?

I balance between my professional obligation as an American soldier to capture or kill the terrorist and my professional obligation as an American soldier to protect the terrorist that we capture. I'm fucked no matter what. So, I choose to report this, and now my rapport with Saedi is strained. But my relationship with Saedi is now the least of my worries.

I suspect that these prisoners were tortured right here in Mosul, in the prison of another Iraqi unit, and then they were sent north to where this torture couldn't be found out. But even more distressing is my suspicion that Americans are somehow involved.

Did another military adviser give tacit approval for this? Did they intentionally look the other way and not report when the torture was so severe? I think so. My guess is that by sending them north, the Iraqis, the Americans, thought the prisoners would be lost in the shuffle of the dozens of prisoners that come and go. That no one would find out.

But they weren't lost. God damn it, I was the one who found out.

And even though he was not directly involved, Saedi's reputation is tarnished and he feels it's my fault for demanding that these prisoners be found and returned.

He's right to feel this way. It would've been easy to not say a thing; nobody would have found out. But what about my other suspicions? Should I tell that I suspect the Americans? God, I feel stretched thin, and completely alone in the world.

Germany, September 2011

10 Days Remain

Crawling in my skin/These wounds, they will not heal/Fear is how I fall/Confusing what is real/There's something inside me that pulls beneath the surface/Consuming, confusing/This lack of self-control I fear is never-ending

I turn the radio down and hand my identification card to the man who guards the entrance to the American base.

This morning, I decided to see a medical doctor; after my talk with the mathematician and my floating ideation, I had to do something.

The guard hands me back my identification card and I walk into the health clinic.

My name is called.

I sit on a medical table.

I describe what is wrong.

I chronicle all my physical ailments.

I want to rule out something physical for my fucked-up thinking.

The doctor takes my temperature and blood pressure and then asks some questions. I describe my headaches, my quakes, my energy and stillness. He takes some blood.

But I know my blood won't show my problems—what I really need is a scan of my head. What I really need is an MRI. A doctor needs to see my brain.

I want to check for that thing that I know must be there, in the center, slowly growing and pressing—a brain tumor would explain everything, which would be a fucking comfort. But what if it's not a lump swelling in the middle of my brain? What if there is nothing physically wrong with me?

—

Two days later, after my doctor's office visit, I hear a ring coming from somewhere. I search the house. I find the phone. I know the answer is coming.

It's the assistant from the doctor's office.

He tells me the blood tests are back.

My cholesterol is the best.

I'm healthy as an ox.

Iraq, 2005

171 Days Remain

. . . I feel really lucky to be here. I mean, where else can one live, work, sleep, eat, and fight insurgents in a different culture, and fight them with other Muslims? Where else can one interrogate "killers" for hours, then open the door to see a beautiful orange sunrise over a flowing river and hear calls for prayer? Where else can one arrive at the scene of a bombing and see a soldier, smiling while holding up the limp Halloween mask of a suicide bomber's face? Where else can this scene be a pleasant surprise? Where else can an unborn child be pulled from a woman's belly, then decapitated? Where else can one be called to help with a car that was shot up, a car where a whole family still sits in their seats, eyes still open but dead? I later found out that a convoy of Americans had thought this car was filled with terrorists. The Americans shot, and then the Americans just kept on going, kept on driving, as fast as they could in order to get safely out of town. I think it was the convoy of a local American general who was going to the Iraqi training base east of the city. The soldiers who drive the general around, like most of the soldiers who live on the American base, seldom come out from behind their razor wire; but when they do, they drive terrified. Strykers, who are always on patrol, wouldn't do this. I hope.

It really pissed me off, but I keep telling myself they just didn't know that they'd killed this family. The Americans are on their big and secure bases, all safe behind the wire in their small America, but they know that just outside is the enemy. They can feel this threat always pressing in, and then they rush out filled with adrenaline and speed, and weave, smash, and shoot through the busy streets filled with shoppers and families and the chance terrorist. American bases cause us to be so out of touch. I know they are scared, but damn! I hate it when Iraqis ask me to account for the shit that other Americans do. An informant talked with me about the death of this family and how this makes him not want to talk. And then next week, maybe two, I'll hear similar words from a prisoner. We'll be in the cell, interrogating, and I'll hear "Americans killed that whole family, why do you think I do what I do? Of course I want to kill Americans."

∽

Amy didn't answer my preplanned call. Should I write her anyway, and tell her a few things—that I love and miss her? I'm a hypocrite. Fuck, this has to end.

There was a large firefight yesterday. The Iraqi police got in a shootout with terrorists in a house; they called the Iraqi Army and Americans, who then came to assist. The house was filled with terrorists, and it was a pretty bad fight all around—some other Special Forces soldiers I know were killed. They tried to enter the house, which was rigged with explosives.

My treadmill broke today. The Iraqis say they can fix it, but I have my doubts. This really upsets me—my runs help me get through the day. I feel the tears well up in frustration, and I've decided that no matter the danger of running outside, I really need to run. But it's just not the same, so now I just run around in a small circle under some trees in a tiny space next to the river. This area provides me some safety from sniper fire. It's a little safer.

This safer tiny area where I now run was once the Guest House's rose garden and swimming pool in the Saddam Hussein era. There are little paths that weave between bushes and around a moldy pool and up some stairs and then passes by the grave of Rocky the dog, our former mascot. He contracted rabies, so we had to shoot him, which was really sad.

This area where I now run is a dystopia, a city park years after a nuclear war with a pool filled with razor wire, and wild dogs growling from overgrown bushes. The beauty echoes as I run a little loop that takes me a minute. I do this loop about thirty times. But it is safe, or at least I think it is, until I hear a few nearby rifle shots. I'm always hearing these sounds, but today these shots threw my pace off.

Tonight, or is it the morning—fuck, who cares—I'm talking with another prisoner, an engineering student, an excellent English speaker, and an insurgent cell leader. He organized his own cell, which he says is not affiliated with al-Qaeda or any former regime elements. He claims to have killed Americans, but most insurgents make this claim. It gives them prestige, respect in the community.

But today the interrogation is different. A few weeks ago, Saedi asked me to come speak with him personally, so today I speak with him by myself, as a fellow human being.

Sometimes an insurgent will come through our door who Saedi thinks is redeemable. His hope is that my interaction with these insurgents will somehow help. So I try, always I try, and two weeks ago I walked into the cell. This insurgent was standing with his back to the wall, and his hands were in plastic flex-cuffs.

I walked in and moved to stand only a foot away from his face.

I could feel the shimmers of hate come off this man, and so I just stared. I needed to decide which path to take . . . and then I say in Arabic . . .

"God bless you. My name is Captain Edmonds. Have you been given water, and have they allowed you time to pray?" He doesn't reply. He just stares at me.

It takes weeks of conversations, not interrogations, and it's an experiment. I want to learn, and I'm persistent. "Teach me," I ask, respectfully; "and can I record our words?"

Now, weeks later, we sit down on flimsy plastic lawn chairs under a large green tree. I sense that things are different—Saedi was right, it seems, about both this prisoner and me.

We talk about his family, about Iraq and this war, and his past job with the 101st Airborne, and why Iraqis kill both Americans and each other. This man then tells me, "I don't hate Americans. I hate the American government, your military." He proclaims, loudly, "You occupy my country and bring democracy with an M-16 rifle. You bring democracy, but the Iraqi pays the price."

Over the next week, this Iraqi tries to explain why he became an insurgent and why he now fights. He talks about a thousand things, about how two years ago he worked on the American base and installed computers, and how his views changed over time until finally he and a couple of friends formed a Mortar Cell to lob bombs at Americans. He says that "almost every minute of my life I hear some noise or see some sight of the American military. You only speak to Iraqis from behind a gun, from a position of power and not respect."

Does this man epitomize why Saedi believes that now only containment of this insurgency is possible, that there is no such thing as a "win"? This insurgent is smart, passionate, unpredictable, and entrepreneurial. Most importantly, he represents a truth that I cannot escape. His words describe a belief I am starting to share: our actions over the decades, over these past years, make this war unwinnable. Have our past deeds, do our current actions, do these things unintentionally create the anger I now see in this man? Did we create this insurgent? I'm conflicted because I'm starting to believe this is true, but then I am having a hard time believing that anything is true anymore.

Iraq, 2005

160 Days Remain

There is a new American unit in charge of Mosul now, and this unit is much better than the old one. They seem to care more about understanding the intangible, non-quantifiable aspects of an insurgency and how these factors should drive their tactics. The old unit was all about killing and capturing insurgents: how many captured, how many killed, how many patrols, how many operations, objectives, and targets. The old unit was good at capturing and killing, there is no denying that, but their actions were simplistic, and fighting an insurgency requires thoughtful people capable of counterintuitive thinking.

As I sit on my roof contemplating, I notice some American advisers who live across town limp into our small base. I make my way down to meet them; their vehicle was hit by an IED. The bulletproof glass was scarred, and there were dents all over. We helped them out, and I looked inside to see what looked like the aftermath of a tornado: stuff thrown all over the place and signs that shrapnel had bounced all around. I was amazed that these advisers only had a few cuts and bruises, but the interpreter sitting in the back seat had been grazed by some shrapnel. I looked and looked and couldn't figure out how this shrapnel had entered the armored vehicle, but then I noticed that the little door in the back had been left open. Behind the back seat is a tiny one-foot-square door where passengers can reach through the armor to access the trunk. They had forgotten to close a little one-foot-square door! Fucking amazing! Amazing to think of the probabilities involved in this attack and the pure luck that is their surviving. Living is chance, not wisdom.

Do I go or not go on patrol? Do I leave now or wait one second, three minutes, ten minutes, or more? Do I test-fire the 50-cal one last time to make sure it works? Do I turn left or right when we exit the front gate? Do I swerve left or right or just go straight under this overpass? Do I look left or right at this intersection? Do I drive by that vehicle that looks innocently parked, or should I change direction? Do I wait in this standstill traffic, or do I crash across a median to drive on the wrong side of the road? Do I scan that rooftop, that door, or which of the hundred alleyways that I pass? Do I shoot, or not, the car that merges suddenly from my right? Do I minutely divert my attention to scratch my nose now, or wait a few seconds more?

So many seemingly insignificant things to decide, and when I'm killed you'll be able to trace my choices in reverse to see the thousands of decisions and how each was the only decision that could have led to my demise. Now I always check that little one-foot-square door.

⌐

I'm trying to share more with Amy. Sharing doesn't seem to help. At least that is how it feels.

I've been trying to catch her on IM, but she is never there. Tonight, I asked her to meet me online at 8 A.M., D.C. time. I'll see if she makes it this time. And then there is our disagreement about Christmas. I am really looking forward to seeing my family, but she says she may not come, and if she does come she will leave early: she needs to go back to the East Coast to spend time with her sister. Two days with me after these seven months of war? I wish she could do more. I was hoping maybe some wine-tasting and a B&B in central California after Christmas. But I tell her I understand if she can't spend more time with me and that she must get back to D.C. But this is not true.

I don't understand.

I am mad, and I guess after she leaves I will just visit my friend Scott in San Luis Obispo, and we'll run trails in the Mountain of Gold.

And then she says she met an Iraqi recently who is both Kurdish and from the same town that Saedi comes from. I asked her to pass me some of his thoughts. Did she? No.

And has she watched any of the movies I've watched and that I've recommended? Probably not. If she has, she hasn't told me. So I tell her I watched another movie that I recommend. What more can I say? That her watching the same movie that makes me cry creates some gossamer bond between us? I'm not sure if this is congruity or synchronicity; but regardless, it means something, at least to me who's out here on the world's edge.

I share things with her; about my growing fascination with the Arabic language, about my fascination with Islam, and about how I am becoming more Iraqi and less myself. So I'm trying, really, but will it make a difference? I doubt it. If not for this isolation, would I still crave this relationship? I'm beginning to think I should break up over Christmas.

～

I shake my dainty porcelain cup and stir the little metal spoon. I am desperate, desperate to remix the half-inch of sugar that has sunk to the bottom. It's been an especially long night and then morning, so I stir and I think about what I'm becoming: disillusioned, disheartened, and cynical, about everything, about the things I am seeing and the things we are doing. About Saedi's "killers" helplessly moaning their innocence? I'm conflicted even about my once-certain righteousness.

As I'm musing melancholy, Saedi is talking and I am thinking about all of the insurgents that bemoan my existence and the informants that won't talk and who say their reason is me, "the American." They say that they won't talk with me and that I am the cause of everything.

I am thinking of the civilians who "tch-tch" at me with raised fingers, accentuating their bitter anger. They are mad at me, always, and lately my talks and my thoughts are consumed by a need to comprehend, to understand them. But I can't seem to shake loose their anger, which hangs like an itchy wool coat over my sunburnt shoulders. . . .

"At the beginning of this war," Saedi begins after a few pleasantries, "before U.S. forces came inside Iraq, some religious men came to my father, who is a tribal leader and also a very smart and religious man. They asked him, 'What do you think if we support jihad against U.S. forces in Iraq?' My father answered, 'If you want to conduct jihad, then you first conduct jihad inside yourself and in your own home. We have so many young men who have strayed from the path, who do not pray or fast. First get them on the straight path. Secondly, you will be a mujahad under whom? You must have a leader for jihad. Third, you must have the base for jihad. Do you have people who support and agree with you? And then most importantly, what are the conditions which give you purpose and justify this jihad? Why do you fight, and what is your goal?'"

"For many insurgents," Saedi tells me, "the belief that your presence is unjust is their purpose and goal, and how you treat most Iraqis is their proof."

I have slowly come to understand that this is the single most important dynamic that fuels the insurgency. Why has it taken me so long to see this? It is absolutely essential that Americans understand this. It is irrelevant whether I agree or disagree with their reasoning, but to be successful I must try to empathize.

Most insurgents who confess during an interrogation attribute their actions to an all-consuming hatred of America. It's become a common theme. In a few cases, this motivation is based on a "true" belief that fighting back is religiously or patriotically justified and that their actions are just and pure. But as long as we persist with our "kill all insurgents" counterinsurgency mentality, this "pure" motivation will only dig itself deeper into the populace's psyche.

When Saedi finishes, my interpreter says: "When I was driving to work today, I drove near where a battle had happened. There was a body of a terrorist with police around it. I heard people saying 'Look, a mujahad,' and their fists were raised."

It's hard for me to comprehend the true power of religion and how deeply ingrained religious principles and philosophies are. I've lost God in this place, but for the Iraqi citizen, the very people who must look away for the insurgency to succeed, the insurgent's religious appeal to jihad resonates. And because of the interrogation, I now realize that America's outsider status cannot be overcome by even the most successful information campaign, selfless act, or altruistic motive. We're past that.

Most insurgents are motivated not because they lack employment or lack an opportunity at an education. It's a factor, but not the real reason they fight. They fight because they resent the occupation of their country by non-Muslim outsiders whom they don't understand, who are interfering, and whose motives are hidden. They fight because their lives are controlled by people who they believe disrespect their religion, culture, and women. Justified or not, I must understand this motivation. Over these last many, many weeks, this need is consuming me.

Many times during an interrogation, Saedi will beg for my forgiveness for things he is about to say. It's at this point where he attempts to establish rapport with the detainee by identifying with insurgents' motives for attacking Americans.

"I hate the Americans," Saedi will say as I stand in the back of the room. "As long as you did not kill Iraqis, tell me about what you have done." Regardless of their opposing roles in this war, identifying with another Muslim against the "common enemy," the American, is sometimes enough, and that is when the insurgent will start bragging.

Today, as I sit in Saedi's office, I recall the countless talks with civilians and insurgents and can't help but see that their hate of me is now dominant and virulent, and it's held with absolute conviction. It won't go away, until I go away. I hope their wish comes true.

Germany, September 2011

7 Days Remain

The trees flash, flash, and flash by me through the train window. In between each flash, I catch a fleeting glimpse of a prison, a man, a face . . . but I can't . . . I can't get away from these images.

Iraq, 2005

152 Days Remain

If all goes according to plan, I will go home for Christmas around the fifteenth and return to Iraq after the New Year, I would suspect after the fifth of January or so.

I had guard duty last night and today is theoretically my day off, so I plan to watch some episodes of *Friends*, study some Arabic, but not much else. But then Saedi gives me a call and so I head over to talk with him. I'm not excited to see him, but it's my responsibility.

"Saedi, can I please have some more of the delicious tea?" I raise my glass, and the Iraqi guard who diligently props up the door runs to pour. I'm in a gracious mood today, as I show by the complimenting of their tea. My interpreter grabs an aerosol can and sprays some tobacco-scented air freshener. Two informants quickly join us, as they always seem to do; it is almost like these informants are mascots and they sit and wait in a hidden room that allows them to always know when I am here. When everyone is seated, Saedi begins to impart some nugget of knowledge, which I'm beginning to detest.

"Okay. Look, Mr. Bill," says Saedi. "Ninety-nine percent of our citizens are not terrorists or terrorist supporters. They go about their daily lives driving their vehicles or walking to buy groceries, visiting friends or relatives, or attending the mosque to pray or to walk to school. However, everyone has at one time or another been shot at or at least had a gun pointed at them. In Mosul, it is common for a father with his family to get too near an American vehicle, to turn a corner and scare an American patrol, or to run a red light and be mistaken for a car bomb. When you meet and get to know them, American soldiers are friendly—sometimes—but when do we get the opportunity to be friends? In their vehicles, they are scared and so shoot first, and these things are making people want to do terrorism."

I look around the room, and my face shows my Americanism. Saedi, the two interpreters, the local imam, the Kurdish police officer, the local muktar, and the two informants who I'm sitting with just stare back. It seems they've decided to gang up on me this evening and to tell me a truth that seems so apparent to them. Their increasing bluntness must be a side-effect of our seven months of constant interaction.

I know their words describe a common Iraqi perception of a very big problem, but I have, until these last few months, not truly understood what they've been trying to tell me. But it has taken seven months of this life, of not being desensitized and inoculated by our large bases and drowning armor and technological superiority, of fighting the same enemy but facing completely different dynamics, to finally *see*. Because of the prism of an Iraqi prison, I've grown a new pair of eyes, and now I comprehend a vastly different perspective.

What they tell me in a thousand different words, gestures, and pleas of understanding, is that our actions, our tactics, and our one-on-one American and Iraqi interactions, are causing a few civilians to turn insurgent and the majority to look away when the few insurgents act. My view has transformed.

When I first arrived on this base and when I first went out on patrol, the sound of two helicopters constantly flying overhead was a comfort. When the two high-flying jets turned on their afterburner? I was comforted. When the Americans on the local base shot their weekly artillery barrage into an open field in the center of town solely to ensure that Iraqis don't forget our presence? I was comforted. When I heard the sound of blaring Stryker horns swerving and crashing through dense city traffic? I was comforted. When I heard the distinctive sound of American gunfire? I was comforted. All American soldiers are comforted by these very characteristic sounds of war. They are the sounds of safety, of security. They are the American comfort blanket, so why wouldn't the Iraqis feel this way?

Now, seven months later, these same comforting sounds have become the persistent and pervasive fingernail-on-a-chalkboard-overwhelming-the-consciousness-of-an-entire-city noise. It pounds on the head of every single person of every single second of every single day and reminds them of a presence that makes them miserable and who they wish they could live without. These sounds are now a painful psychic probe; I am no longer comforted.

Now, I jump when the artillery unexpectedly goes off unannounced. I feel disgust at our puerile need to fire random barrages of artillery in the middle of a city; shooting artillery at nothing in the center of the city! Stupid fucks! I cringe at the blaring of Stryker horns and the sound of their gunfire; I know sometime soon a civilian will comment to me on some senseless death they saw or some senseless act that was done to them. I have become desensitized to the supremacy of our military power and sensitized to nuances of how our military power is ironically causing us to lose this war. I am seeing that the efficacy of every single American policy, military tactic, personal interaction must be judged by this metric; by its positive effect on the civilian. And if a second- or third-order effect is to capture or kill an insurgent?

Great! But that should never be our first-order reason for any counterinsurgent operation.

My reaction is indicative of a drastic eye-opening and is also a very disturbing change of feeling. Is this what these Iraqis have tried to explain to me for so long? Am I becoming more like them and less like my former self?

I know some will think these changes, my words, mean I have "gone native," that I'm the mirror image of Stockholm Syndrome. And I would say: "Damn right, I am conflicted!" But how we act is based on how they see the world, so how can I win a counter-insurgency without going native?

"Here, Mr. Bill. Read this Iraqi news service," says the Muktar as he passes over a piece of paper:

U.S. TROOPS OPENED FIRE AT A CIVILIAN VEHICLE AS IT PASSED BY AL-HADBA NEIGHBORHOOD IN THE WESTERN PART OF MOSUL, NORTHERN IRAQ. THE THREE OCCUPANTS OF THE VEHICLE WERE MARTYRED IN THE INCIDENT. AL-SHAQIYAH'S CORRESPONDENT CITED SOURCES AT THE CITY POLICE AND FORENSIC MEDICINE AS SAYING THE U.S. TROOPS HAD SUSPICIONS ABOUT THE VEHICLE AND OPENED FIRE, HITTING THE THREE OCCUPANTS—A MAN, A WOMAN, AND A CHILD—IN DIFFERENT PARTS OF THEIR BODIES, WHICH CAUSED THEIR IMMEDIATE DEATH. THE U.S. FORCES, HOW-EVER, DID NOT MAKE ANY COMMENT ON THE INCIDENT.

"These suspicious people?" the muktar continues. "These people were from my neighborhood."

Then the Iraqi police officer makes a comment: "There is an Iraqi who works with us. Yesterday, a second relative of his was killed by Americans. Both of these relatives came too close to a Stryker."

Yes, I know, for only a few weeks ago the brother of my interpreter was killed by Americans as well. He was just collateral damage. I spent weeks trying to figure out how to get my interpreter some compensation—and if this was difficult for me, I can't even imagine what this is like for them. And yes, I know that these deaths were probably within the military's rules of engagement, but this fact is irrelevant so I don't even bother to say it.

Having relatives and close family members die can only have a negative impact on the perceptions of these citizens. The impact of such instances is even greater in a tribal society, where a person counts close relatives in the hundreds and sometimes thousands. Shit, what would my reaction be if it were my brother, my sister, my daughter, my mother, or father? Would I lob some mortars as well? Fuck yes, I would. I would sow terror. I would become my own worst nightmare.

And don't even get me started at our penchant for night raids. Yes, these are important. This is when lazy terrorists sleep in comfortable beds. But here, now, in Mosul, for every terrorist we capture, a whole neighborhood is traumatized. An insurgent I captured, another one of my "experiments," once spoke at length with me on this subject. In effect he said that the capture of a terrorist within the city should always be of secondary importance. What is a priority? First, any operation should be viewed as an opportunity for Americans to come out from their bases and from behind their armor, to get within a neighborhood, where they can finally go from house to house acting respectfully. And that terrorist in a house? Well, great, if we capture or kill him, but the primary reason for our operations should be to change people's perspectives. When we leave a neighborhood, there is only one measure of success: Do the residents feel better, or worse?

Even if all people were supporters of America to begin with, I know that even the friendliest person would begin to resent weapons pointed at their family. These people start to look away when they see insurgents kill Americans. And again, "looking away" is "tacit support," and this is all that is needed for America to lose. Fuck, just look at the downward glide path of this war:

from cheering the liberator to killing the oppressor. Using hundreds of thousands of young soldiers to counter an urban insurgency? God, we are just so stupid.

I hate that I am starting to see the truth of their words. I hate that I am seeing the world through their eyes. It is even more disconcerting to realize that maybe their version of the truth is truer than mine. "American soldiers either deliberately or unintentionally treat Iraqis, all Iraqis, like second-class citizens. The closest analogy," says the Iraqi policeman in the corner, "is the blacks in your country. Think of how African Americans were treated by White Americans in your country. Not when they were slaves, but in this century. This is how civilians feel when they are around American soldiers. In most cases, American soldiers do not even acknowledge the presence of an Iraqi unless that Iraqi initiates conversation."

I remember back to the conversation I'd had with another "experiment." "I love Americans but hate your army. Two years ago, I saw Abu Ghraib and what Americans did to women; I became an insurgent. You come into our homes without separating the women and children, or asking the men politely if you may enter. Almost every hour of my life, I hear some noise or see some sight of the American military. Last week American soldiers got on a school bus and talked with all of the teenage girls. You had them take off their hijabs so you could see their faces! You do not respect our women! This is the biggest of all problems of yours; you do not respect our women."

But it is not just how we deal with their women: it is how we interact with every Iraqi as an individual. Almost every single insurgent leader's ability to recruit and sustain a cell can be linked back in some direct or indirect way to the effect of these perceptions on the civilian population. Almost every single insurgent's ability to survive and fight can be linked back in some direct or indirect way to an Iraqi's response to how we treat them, from our policies, to our strategies, to our tactics, and lastly to our one-on-one interactions between American soldiers and Iraqi civilians. The percentage of soldiers who work actively to change this perception is small. How can they? They rarely come out from their bases to walk on their God-given two feet, so they are unable to overcome the many assumed, false, and truthful stereotypes that are associated with us. We continually prove we are the Ugly American.

"I have conducted over forty mortar attacks on American bases in the last two years," a detainee recently told me. "I do this from within the neighborhoods, in between the houses, with Iraq civilians living, working, and playing. Could I do this, over such a long time, if it were not true that most Iraqis hate Americans?"

Germany, September 2011

7 Days Remain

. . . but still they flash, flash, flash by . . . I keep staring out the window while the past flashes by. And I can't flee, so the reflection speaks to me:

"What comes first, the chicken or the egg?"

"Only the chicken acted intention" I scream. "But if you want to assign guilt, it's the fucking wrong question."

Iraq, 2005

145 Days Remain

I sent a few e-mails and I tried calling a few times, but I still haven't heard from Amy in over two weeks. I hope everything is all right, but I have my doubts. Something is going on.

This morning I just lay around in bed, staring at the ceiling, and unable to get up. Something is going on. I feel lazy and lethargic. I have been lazy a lot lately, so this morning I decide to give in and just lie there, staring at the ceiling over my head. I've never really had a reason to just stare at the ceiling above my bed.

At the start of the Iraq war, the Guest House used to be a small American base, used by the 101st Division, I think; and as I lie in my bed, looking up, I see etched into the ceiling the anger and distress of those American soldiers from years past. Their words are scratched right there, scratched in black, right over my head: *"The mind is a terrible thing," "keep a sharp lookout during your descent," "happiness is a temporary state of mind," "control is just an illusion,"* and *"nothing is as it seems."* Across the room, on another wall, are other words from another soldier. They read, *"My score in this War: Arabs=10, cars=10, houses=3."*

As I lie in this bed, I can't help but wonder where these young, angry, and confused soldiers are right now. I'm sure it wasn't too long ago that they etched these words in my ceiling; but wherever they are, I now interrogate the consequence of their anger.

It's now the second week of December, and I leave for Christmas break in one week. Amy writes and says she doesn't want to talk. I tell her I will be here when she is ready. I tell her I would love to listen; but frankly, would I really? I honestly don't think so. I go back and forth on whether we should stay together, and more and more I realize that I am not that conflicted any more about our relationship. Iraq's provided me the needed distance to see that we're close to the end. So I close the e-mail from Amy and leave the TOC to get ready for our patrol.

Today we drive around Mosul, to end up on the other side of town to have lunch with another unit of the Iraqi Army. We all stand up, gathered around tables to eat some type of rice with chunks of fatty lamb, a tomato-based vegetable stew that's mostly eggplant, and some flat bread. It's not particularly appetizing. For the Iraqis, maybe, but not for me. Living here, I know what goes on, and this knowledge ruins my appetite.

Hundreds squat over a single hole with splatters of shit every-where, use their hands to clean themselves, and then barely wash their hands, if at all. Then they prepare the food I eat. It gets really hard to actually eat, so today I just nibble and push my food around in circles. I haven't had a hard shit in eight months, and eight months of runny shit is mentally and physically exhausting. Trust me on this.

But you get used to it, almost, or at least you just deal with it. I mean, what choice do I have? For me, the hardest thing to deal with is the knowledge of where the food comes from. Every house in the city throws the trash out the front door. This trash is then pushed into bigger piles, which eventually make their way to a large pile on a street corner. Then, all across the city are herds of sheep, roaming and grazing on these steaming wallows of human waste. These sheep gorge themselves to become fatter and fatter, and then they transform to become the slab of pure fat that wallows in the melted fat on my plate. And when I am done, my food scraps go out the back door to be thrown on the top of another steaming pile of waste and then soon, over time, this pile becomes a bigger pile on a street corner. A herd of sheep finds and then grazes . . . which becomes the meat I eat . . . this existence is a sick and twisted version of the circle of life!

And then there is the sewage from the two million people that travels downhill to eventually become ten feet of bowel sludge on the bottom of the Tigris. Big ugly mutated fish roam with open and bulging lips to eventually suck in a hook. An Iraqi soldier goes out to buy this manure-filled bottom-sucking behemoth, which then becomes my evening meal. I stand there. I look down. Beads of sweat travel down my forehead. My mouth is dry. I can't swallow. But I force myself to jostle my dirty fingers with fifty other unwashed digits as we all grope around this communal plate. I pinch together mashed up fish and pull it slowly toward my quivering lips. Sweat stings my averted eyes. I smile and then close my eyes. I swallow.

I open my eyes to see the flies, everywhere, land on every piece I reach out to grab. As I shoo these flies away, grease and saliva are flung in every direction to land back on the communal plate. God. It's so hard to eat this shit. Yet I force myself to, just a bit, but tonight's meal seems to have upset my stomach, so I run to the Iraqi bathroom with ass cheeks clenched vacuum-tight. It's not a pretty sight. . . .

Today I fly home for Christmas break. Tomorrow I'll be in a relationship. In some ways I'd rather just stay here and not have to deal with it. I should be excited, yet I dread this break more than I fear just staying here.

Iraq, 2006

137 Days Remain

Amy and I broke up over Christmas, and now I'm back in Iraq. It's a new start of a New Year.

I hope it was the right decision. Life just took us down different paths, and I began to see a future where turning around was impossible. The breakup with Amy was harder than I expected, but fortunately I have Iraq, and I can just dive back into the fight. But I can't help thinking that it was my fault, and that I have some inability to be happy. Am I completely unrealistic in my expectations of harmony, of wanting something that just "clicks," where there is no constant conflict? Who *doesn't* want this? But screw self-pity. I have more important things to worry about.

I need to make a decision. I need to work out where I stand.

On my way to California to spend Christmas with my family, I traveled through Washington, D.C. While there, I stopped by the Pentagon and spoke with a general, someone who I know and respect. I went to his Pentagon office and told him about my dilemma, about the prisoner torture that I had uncovered and how I suspect Americans. He advised that I do what is right, regardless of the consequences—"do all you can to uncover the truth, and tell the truth."

So now I'm back in Iraq, and once again I am not sure what to do. Should I report or stay silent? Was it more wrong to torture these killers or to let these killers go free? Damn it, it's so fucking complex, and this inner conflict is destroying me . . . morality is not binary! It's not black and white. My choices just . . . well, depend.

So as I sit on my roof and watch the sun descend, I reach out to touch the wind: "Is torture wrong or right?" But, shit, I have to use logic to answer my question; emotion only confuses me.

First I will define my terms: Is torture "the infliction of unbearable physical and mental pain in order to coerce a person or to attain pleasure"? I've tried a hundred definitions, and every single one seems to include subjective terms; in this case "unbearable," which, according to Webster, "unbearable" is the opposite of "capable of being borne." So must I expand my definition with an explanation of these subjective statements, such as: "What is the opposite of 'capable of being borne?' And then these explanations include subjective terms. Defining the subjective leaves no end!

How can I possibly argue with myself when the topic is indefinable? It seems that torture is like porn; I will know it when I see it. If this reasoning is good enough for the Supreme Court, it's good enough for me.

"So, what's my second line of inquiry?" I ask. "Whom do I interrogate?"

There are two fundamental categories: the Guilty, and the Innocent. Other categorizations only confuse the issue. And then there are two types of information that I seek, and which both the Innocent and Guilty provide me: information for the Confession, and information used for more and better Intelligence. But is "Intelligence" a justification? Day in and day out, I increasingly become less confident of coerced information. Soldiers go on missions based on this information. Are they risking their lives on Intelligence I believe is often unreliable?

So, what's left? Justify torture for the sake of a Confession? Is torture justified to gain a Confession, which will then hopefully put a killer behind bars and thus stop him from killing again? Am I willing to torture a person to get information I already know? Am I torturing them just to obtain confirmation? I need to try something else.

There are two arguments for, and against, torture: these are "moral" and "utility": the "right action" versus the "effective action." I'll start with the "moral" justification, but then I realize almost every opinion on this topic is uninformed and any person can argue any moral position in order to stay convinced of a particular faith. Just look at the common use of the "ticking time bomb scenario." I've stood on the banks of the Tigris and pulled, and pulled, and pulled on this thread, and every time I pull myself to an almost theoretically impossible and unverifiable scenario. Damn it, it presumes knowledge of cause and effect I just don't have. If almost every opinion is uninformed, if any person can argue any moral position, does this make "morality" an ineffective measure for the "right" or "wrong" of torture? Does this same reasoning apply to my use of "utility" as a measure?" I am going in circles and getting nowhere.

But I also have to admit that this is such bullshit, this sitting on a rooftop using "logic" to determine "right action." Ethical codes only rationalize what people want to do, and I won't evade personal responsibility. In the end the only choice I can make is the one I can live with. Only I own my decisions.

And I don't care if there are U.S. government memos, DoD studies and Secretary of Defense comments, and secret "black sites," which imply—no, which tell me—that the "mere infliction of pain and suffering is not unlawful," that Human Interrogation Technique #16 can be presidentially authorized. I don't care that my own government gives me a "pass" and says that when it comes to terrorists, the Geneva Conventions do not apply. Why?

Because an authority's license, no matter how implicit, incentivizes a collective moral slide. When my government says—or implies—"you can," it's only a few steps before it becomes "I will" and this isn't a hypothetical that I am in: it's real. Damn real. Because regardless of my excuses to ignore what I know is right,

I am overwhelmed by the atrocity and the inhumanity of these killers and here, in these cells, I have the power to stop them. And I'm morally wrong when I do, and when I don't.

I now realize that I am just trying to use logic to convince myself that wrong is right, that black is white, and that torture is justified. But I know every single argument, and it's so easy to convince myself that Saedi is right, that I am right, that these prisoners are guilty horrible people who don't deserve any sympathy or mercy, that they have information that could save a life, that they deserve justice. It would be so easy to say that I don't have the luxury of civility, that a confession would put them behind bars, and that torture would stop them from killing again.

But I also realize that my arguments exert on me a relentless pull to continually lower my bar. I start with "okay, screw with them mentally." Then it becomes a "slap is okay, but nothing more." Then my bar lowers even more when even worse killers come through my door. Soon it becomes: "If I know this person is a killer, then anything I do to stop him is justified—torture will save an innocent life." But where am I willing to stop? There is no logical end to this reasoning! I will always be able to convince myself that I am right, that this killer is guilty and in "this case" torture is necessary, that it is justified. But God damn it! I know that this is such bullshit, because I've *seen* and I *know* how torture is always the immoral choice.

This understanding is not hypothetical: it is empirical. I daily witness these mental gymnastics, and I constantly force myself to stand in the way of my own, and of others', descent into a moral abyss. And some days I lose these arguments. I'm afraid of where I'll go, and that I've lost myself.

For me, the final metric for any discussion of "right" and "wrong" is this: Am I willing to hurt another person in order to prove the preconceptions of fallible people? And the level of "torture" or "pressure" or "techniques" only increases until those preconceptions are proven true. Most of the time, I think I'm right, and when the future proves me true, I personally believe torture can be the less wrong action to take—that torture is wrong, but by not torturing I am allowing an even worse atrocity to occur. But even then, I am able to identify all of my own preconceptions in this logic. If I were to remove the conditional clause in my reasoning, would I still be right? Am I willing to chance the torture of an innocent to hypothetically save another innocent? Am I willing to risk every negative consequence because the absence of evidence proves I am right and the longer my faith remains hidden, the more pressure I feel necessary to apply?

Do I use torture to prove a negative? Am I absolutely certain of my own infallibility? Am I God? No, God is not here. I am not God. I'm human, and absolute certainty is certain proof of my absolute ignorance. I need only point to humanity's countless atrocities—to the Inquisition and Nazism—to prove this. I have to only look around at my present—to Islamic Fundamentalism and my government's and my many justifications to torture—to verify this.

But my reasoning only addresses the moral side of my inner struggle. How about the dominant utilitarian that is in me? Yes, torture sometimes works, but it is the last refuge of the incompetent.

More effective is perfecting the battle of wits, knowing every personal detail of the prisoner, being a subject-matter expert on the topic of discussion, controlling every atmospheric nuance, having a plan, and then building a relationship with a prisoner, a relationship that entices the killer to talk.

Put an arm around a shoulder and pretend respect; sometimes even empathy works with these fucking horrible people.

And for the interrogator who is unwilling? These people will always resort to torture—it's easy and emotionally gratifying . . . because I know, fuck I know how it is, how hard it is to not break character, ever, and yes, how it's inhumanely difficult to not lash out at the evil I control. But I know it's possible. It has to be, because I know the world I want. I create it with each and every choice, and this version of the world is not the version I choose to live in.

Iraq, 2006

120 Days Remain

I no longer want my coffee, my Arabic, to interact with Americans, or to even talk with the Iraqis. I'm tired. We went on another patrol yesterday, and I was the gunner. I seek out this job, and fantasize about hitting an IED.

It's now drizzling and cold, everything is wet, muddy, and even the piles of steaming and smoking trash have gone dormant and are unable to burn. The trash is piling up and, because I no longer have a treadmill, my early-morning runs traverse through the stink—once, twice, three times, four, five laps around this horrible base in this horrible place. The wild dogs have moved on; even they no longer have the will to whine from the bushes.

I feel desperately thin and sad—good and bad, right and wrong, ugly and beautiful, distinct colors and clear sounds—all these extremes now just blend together. But then there are times when I sit on the roof and see the clouds part and the sun shine through, and during these few and fleeting moments I can see. This city is dark and sinister but sometimes, if you look really hard, there is a beauty; the minarets that rise into the sky, the ruins of ancient buildings, and the Tigris flowing by with water buffalo feeding. Natural thoughts devoid of people sometimes make sad thoughts shrink to corners. But not today. Not any longer.

I am tired and I need someone to talk with, but there are only the Iraqis, the few Americans, and then myself—standing on a roof, thinking about Amy, my death, those eight prisoners who were horribly tortured: those burns, knife cuts, broken bones, electrical burns, and welts from slashing cables.

I know Saedi and I weren't directly responsible, but God damn it! Those other prisons are my responsibility, and it became my responsibility when I found out, since I came to believe Americans were somehow culpable.

And it took too long for me to decide to demand an investigation. But eventually I did. Fuck, I'm such a pussy.

I e-mailed, called, and talked with so many people over many weeks and months; I talked until my face turned blue and my voice and heart were sore. There were some who listened, but nobody wanted to act on my words. I even wrote my hero, Senator McCain. If there was ever someone who could understand, it would be him. But he never responded. Is every face a facade?

Finally, after weeks, then months, an investigation was ordered. Then what happened? Well, of course everyone is cleared, and now I feel fucking filthy.

But I understand why this happened. There is just so much other bad shit going on for leaders to care. American soldiers are dying, every single day, everywhere, so why should leaders focus on this small thing? My suspicions are only a distraction. "A couple of terrorists are tortured? There are larger more pressing concerns, Captain Edmonds." Do we only care about right and wrong when it becomes a media story?

Was I right to force an investigation, to expose myself like this?

For what seems an entire life I've struggled over what's "right" when "fighting" wrong. And fuck! I know I'll have to account for the countless sins during my search in a pitch-black world. And

God help me! Because I still so desperately want to torture, to kill, these evil people: I can already feel Purgatory stalking me. But I have never done what I uncovered and then covered it up by vanishing them! And then this? I finally sensed a light in the distance and then I find out that no one gives a shit? So much heartache for no purpose. I know terrible things happen every second of every day, everywhere in this world; but on this base, reality seems condensed and comes at me in a thick and steady pour. With every breath I suffocate.

220 Days Remain: Two Iraqi girls from the neighborhood of al-Sukar
One day on a patrol, two little girls smiled but refused the candy I handed out? The world
no longer responded the way it was supposed to.

204 Days Remain: Iraqi guards waiting for new prisoners
Huge changes were happening: Why did I care more about why these killers fought, and less about how to get their confession? The Iraqis didn't have this inner conflict. But I did, and I was terrified; through the window of interrogations I glimpsed a future where we wouldn't win the war. In that future, the killing just kept repeating. I saw it, and I was powerless to stop it.

197 Days Remain: Sitting with Saedi

I tried to find diversions from an increasingly overwhelming reality. I categorized my music collection, obsessively exercised, binge-watched TV series, or spent nights sitting on the bumper of my vehicle—Saedi would talk on the phone with informants while I memorized Arabic conjunctions. But time stretched out before me, and with the slow-motion tick of each second, a new "killer" arrived to interrogate.

191 Days Remain: A killer's daughter brought in for the interrogation
I had no choice but to continue moving forward; every piece of information, each confession, was one less dead American. But one day I asked myself: Did she know her father was our prisoner? I told myself that her life was better this way, but my convincing felt selfish, and desperate.

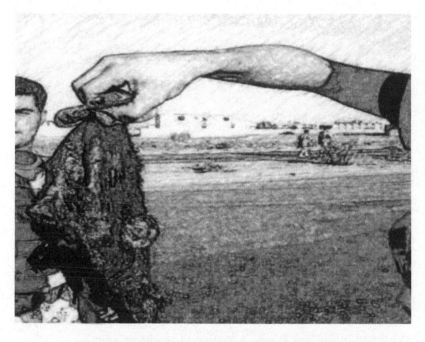

171 Days Remain: Iraqi holding the head of a suicide bomber
One day I woke up and felt the exhilaration of a city. There was eagerness in the air,
and I was lucky to be there. Where else could I hear a killer plead for God's comfort,
and then open the door to a beautiful sunrise and hear muezzins cry "God Is Great!"
With each breath I would suffocate.

160 Days Remain: Author speaking with an insurgent

Saedi felt he was redeemable—that this insurgent was a good person who could be turned. So for weeks we conversed. We just sat and talked, and soon he transformed; he saw that his hate was misguided, and that leaders used him for hidden selfish purposes.

152 Days Remain: Captured terrorist waiting

But every day was just another day where I had to make a soul-crushing decision—do I allow torture, or not—and every day, over and over again, no matter the choice, I made the wrong choice. And then I had no choice but to just live with the life-and-death consequences. It wasn't like I could just go home and run away from a nation's responsibility that had become my own.

137 Days Remain: Back from Christmas break and another operation

Before descending into the basement, I climbed to the roof and had a conversation with myself: It's hard to not break character, to not lash out at the evil you control. But it's possible. It has to be. You create the world with each choice and the world where torture is right is not the world I choose to live in. And for the person who chooses the moral abyss? Those people will always resort to torture—it's the easiest and most emotionally gratifying choice.

102 Days Remain: A new group arrives

But the days wore on, and the stresses of war accumulated and compounded. Soon, I was surrounded. I had to stop interrogating. But evil wouldn't disappear if I chose to look away. The guilty and innocent were still abused, or not. And innocent lives were still lost, or not, as a consequence. But I had to do something. Every day, new prisoners arrived, and soon I would know each soul as intimately as my own.

Iraq, 2006

88 Days Remain

I've decided to stop interrogating, to stop talking with these people. Daily they file in from the streets, and when I enter the cell, I feel the pull to slide down their rabbit hole; they consume me.

They just sit there, only a hundred feet away, the men I want to hurt and the killers I need to kill. Lately, every day I feel this need, so every day I must get away, I must distance myself from myself—I cannot become what I despise, but sometimes it feels as if this has already happened. If I am right, if I am a good person, why do I constantly feel such guilt and shame for the things I don't do? Why do I feel weak for all of my choices? I have the power to make a difference. So why don't I? Every day another killer is let loose, and then the day becomes just another day where I've taken innocent life.

Iraq, 2006

60 Days Remain

I broke down and called Amy tonight. She was drunk.

I understand her desire to escape; I feel this same need, the need for nothingness. I want to sink, and to then fall asleep, or to walk outside my gate and wander aimlessly. But I won't. I have to get home.

Today is colder than ever. There is ice on top of the pools of standing sewage, and I walk around with my jacket always on. I've stopped running. I wish my treadmill was working.

Then there is Amy, who still has control of my house and my finances, and even though we've broken up, she still lives in my condo that I'm paying for, at least until I return. She has my power of attorney. On my short trip home over Christmas, I didn't have time to tie up all the loose ends. I had no other option but to depend on her to take care of everything, all that I own. What happens to me if she becomes vengeful? So I ask her, "Please tell me what is going on." Fuck! Just tell me that everything I own but can't control is still mine. Please tell me that you will not try to get revenge, that you'll not hurt me? Please, I need just one less worry.

Iraq, 2006

38 Days Remain

It's cold, fucking colder than I would have ever imagined it could be. There's ice on the ground and frost on the bushes. I still don't feel like talking—to anyone—or studying, or writing. I am alone most of the time now. I like to just stand behind the door that opens onto my rooftop. I stare out of the rusted iron bars that once held glass. These bars feel like my prison, and I miss the human connection of the interrogation. I know that by not being there, by not taking responsibility, bad things are happening. I hate myself for giving up.

Iraq, 2006

13 Days Remain

It's been almost one year and tomorrow I leave the Guest House to travel through Baghdad, Kuwait, and then to D.C.

Tomorrow begins the journey to a dream.

I came to Iraq loathing Muslims and Islam. I leave with more complex, and nuanced, feelings. I've learned Arabic, made hundreds of Iraqi friends, and understand the basic tenets of Islam. I tell myself I was successful and that I stopped terrorists. I tell myself I saved lives. But at what cost? Do the ends justify becoming a monster?

It's been a year of searing change. I now see evil behind every virtuous façade. Will blissful clarity ever return again?

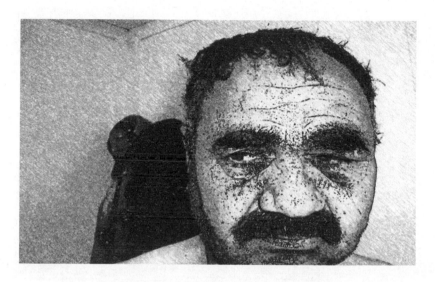

88 Days Remain: The Last Interrogation

My mind slowed as I neared the end. Then I stopped interacting with everyone. I stopped studying Arabic. I stopped interrogating. And then I just . . . stopped. I shut down. I had become the person I hated, and the killer I hated had become a person. The universe's immutable laws became breakable.

**(13 Days Remain) The author looking at Mosul
through his rooftop door's window**
I left Iraq seeing evil behind every virtuous façade, every person and God.

Washington D.C.

0 Days Remain

I've tried to push Iraq away, to hide from my memories. But it's different. Everything feels wrong. There is no blissful clarity here.

I sit and stare out the window at the people and cars coming and going along Connecticut Avenue. I walk the streets and jump at loud noises. I go to fancy restaurants and sit on bar-stools and read magazines to myself. At Bardeo, a local bar, a lady sat down next to me and she thought it was weird that I was at a bar reading and didn't want to talk. I put together a book filled with my best pictures from Iraq and then used it to strike up conversations with complete strangers. I tried to make my book look professional so that Tryst, a local coffee shop, would consider hanging the photos on their wall. They said "No. Too political." There are so many rules; red lights and crosswalk signals, grocery lines and traffic, two-way streets with medians you can't cross, all of which just pisses me off. Rules? For the last year, the only rules I followed were my own. A horrible world doesn't get to define right and wrong. Fuck rules and the world.

Yesterday, I went out for crab with a girl named Cheryl and couldn't take the crunching, breaking, and insides showing, so I got up and left and couldn't explain why. I smile and make eye contact with all the people coming and going, and they either think I am gay or they look away, and sometimes I even notice that they anticipate me—they think I'm strange—and pretend to unintentionally look away. I don't understand these people and their mindless chatter about all the traffic cameras, or how the condo newsletter is late or about how horrible the mosquitoes are this year. "Can you believe a chain restaurant opened up in our neighborhood?" they say in dismay.

I want to respond with my knowledge of the horror that is the human race with all its depravities and hatreds. I want them to understand how easy it is, to reach slowly, or quickly, across a worn and dirty table. How easy it is to take life, to make evil people go away. I remember that man whose malice was so palpable and how easy it would have been to kill him. It would have been so easy and no one who cared would ever have known and the world would be a better place if I had. I know everyone would loathe me for such an act; but if they had the power and responsibility to act, they would do the same thing. Down deep I know they would. It makes me sick that I wanted to kill that man and that it took every fiber of my being to resist. There were so many of these thoughts. Were these my existential moments? Were these right actions? Did I do right?

Screw fiction; reality is what's depressing and entertaining.

Germany, September 2011

0 Days Remain

The rush of thoughts and emotions has slowed, but this absence just feels empty, and lonely, and I'm drinking more than I would like. I don't exercise anymore, and the days now blur together. In fact, I no longer do much of anything; what happened to all the things I once enjoyed? I know that toughing it out, sucking it up, trying hard, and all of those manly things just haven't helped. I'm afraid for my family.

So, today at work, I break down and decide to seek out some professional help. I finally decide to go see Behavioral Health, and I am scared to death what this admission of weakness will mean. But there are more important things to consider than just me. For my family, I have to get better . . . I just leave work and drive across Germany to seek help at Landstuhl Army Medical Center.

I just drop in to the Behavioral Health unit and say "I need help and need to talk to someone."

"Do you have an appointment?" they respond.

I say "No."

"Is this an emergency?" they ask. "Do you want to hurt yourself or your family?"

And I say "No," then sit down to fill out a questionnaire with lots and lots of blank little bubbles. I turn it in and thirty minutes later I go in to talk with a distracted mental health professional. She says that since I didn't have an appointment and since I don't want to hurt myself or someone else, I can't just "drop in." I need to make an appointment.

"There is an opening in fourteen days," she sighs, and says it would be better to see the clinic closer to where I live. But she offers to listen for a few minutes, "if you really want to talk." But I can tell that I am a distraction. So I leave, but before I go I remember to ask the teenaged Army private at the reception desk for the telephone number of the other Health Clinic. The soldier says to call them to make an appointment.

~

During the drive home from Landstuhl I dial the number the high-schooler gave me.

"Are you having suicidal thoughts," they ask, "or do you want to hurt your family?"

"No," I say, "but I am still having problems. I really need to speak with somebody."

"We have an opening in seventeen days," they say.

"No. I need to talk now," I demand.

"Okay. Come in. We'll see if we can fit you in."

PROLOGUE

Behavioral Health Clinic: Germany 2011

Day 0: Continued

The counselor makes a "Hmmm."

The noise comes out of nowhere.

It's out of place and surprises me.

Then my eyes open to see a man in a chair perched over a carpeted floor and I look up to see a poster on the wall, several posters on *Determination, Inspiration, Teamwork,* and *Confidence.* These were hanging here when I began talking, just a moment ago.

My mind adjusts . . . the door closed . . . my eyes shut . . . to wait for an exit opening. . . . Now I remember. I glance at my watch; I've been talking for an hour and ten minutes? But it feels like I've been traveling through a year, over months, and into weeks, minutes, and then seconds, about Iraq and about these last thirty days in September 2011, when everything came back in a second.

It's been a long talk and my throat is dry—I cough.

The counselor leans back, legs crossed. He's a detached unemotional professional and he references the sheet of #2 pencil filled-in bubbles. This is how he understands me.

"So what's going on?" I ask.

"Nothing" he responds.

Nothing?

Damn it, I refuse to force myself on this man, I will not rape him. So I ask again: "Nothing?"

"No. You show indicators, but you don't fit the profile. You just can't handle your stress. I know you're having a hard time, but there's no reason to feel this way. You're okay. If you want, we have a Stress Management Class. And continue your writing. Writing can't hurt. Listen to relaxing music and do some deep-breathing exercises. But I don't think we need to talk anymore."

"Fuck you," I think.

But instead I say "Thanks."

I stand up.

I go home.

I wake up.

I go to work.

And I decide that it's probably best if I tell my supervisor about all that is going on. I tell him that I went to see a mental health counselor, about what we spoke about, and that I will attend a few Stress Management Classes, and about all of my writing. I tell him how I've been writing about my experiences and how the counselor says I should continue. How it may help.

But he doesn't believe me. He thinks I'm malingering.

"What is the name of the person you're speaking with?" my supervisor asks. "What is his name and telephone number? I will call to check and see if this is true. And I think you need to talk with Security. Seeing Mental Health will definitely affect your security clearance. And about that writing? Have you used a government computer or printer? If you have, that can't be legal. I'm going to talk with the lawyer."

I just stand up and leave.

And over the next few weeks they make my life a living hell.

I am a security concern.

I am unprofessional.

I'm drama.

They find every possible way to make me fucking miserable. More miserable than I already am.

Finally, they give me a subtle hint: "Find a new job elsewhere. Just go away quietly and this won't reflect on your performance evaluation."

~

The Next Morning: 1:27:48 A.M.

Another morning, another dream . . . and then Ava starts to cry again, so I jump out of bed to rush in and soothe her. I could tell by her cry, I thought by her cry that it was her tummy or her tooth or maybe she had a bad dream about a very scary subject. I needed to get in fast before her distress became overwhelming. What she needed was a "snap" to distract her from an increasingly overwhelming reality. I sang and sang loud close to her ear, "twinkle twinkle little star how I wonder what you are . . ." and Ava hears, and she understands. She begins to make her little sucking noises that mean she is mentally feeding, which is emotionally soothing. I gently lay her back down and I quietly tiptoe out of her room and crawl back into bed with Cheryl . . .

. . . and I wake up again.

It is still really early. Still too early, and Cheryl is worried, so I get up.

"Where are you going?" she mumbles from under the comforter.

"Downstairs," I answer.

"Are you coming back?"

How did she know?

"I'll be back, I promise, just not right away," I tell her, but really I don't know.

Why? Because I was just lying in bed with my eyes wide but shut. I was, once again, overwhelmed by such a massive flow of thoughts that I could not sleep, deep thoughts with even deeper meanings. Listen to myself! A "deeper meaning"? Me? But it is true. I just feel it. Because if you *truly* knew me, you would know that what I think, more importantly, what I really feel is trapped somewhere deep under my surface. I just have been unable, for a long time, to express it. Why is this happening? Why has an intensely emotional man who lives behind a mask of reason suddenly writing in a journal at 2:05:24 A.M., a journal entry about why people just don't understand? Why am I overwhelmed by thoughts, insights, emotions, and then have unexplained intuitive leaps that flow according to the laws that govern the path of a water drop sliding down a misted window in an open meadow at dawn? Why has my reality suddenly altered from a few shades of gray to a kaleidoscope of infinitely different and bright colors? Why do the words that seem to flow so easily now, and which make absolute sense, later seem the ravings of a socially awkward, angry, and definitely brittle man? Why can I no longer make a human connection? I don't know the "why" to these changes; but the miracle is that if it were not for the love of my family, I would be lost in some inner-city, rocking and mumbling under my breath, desperately trying to describe a never-ending journey of backing through a side door into consciousness. Or I would be dead.

But I have faith, I always have faith that things will get better, and that same faith is still inside, somewhere. So I will write my way through this. And even now I can sense a faint and distant light up ahead. An exit? I hope so. It's been a long and lonely journey—tangled, rough, and savage. God, I want to arrive.

Midway on our life's journey, I found myself
In dark woods, the right road lost. To tell
About those woods is hard—so tangled and
rough
And savage that thinking of it now, I feel
The old fear stirring...

—Dante Alighieri, Inferno, Canto I

EPILOGUE

3 Years after September 2011

Central Africa

The clock whispers 4 A.M.: time for The Ritual to begin.

I need just a few seconds to find the discipline, to slowly roll out from bed and fumble in the dark for the clothes I'd set out the night before.

When dressed, I make coffee: dark roast in a French press. Carrying my cup, I weave around the kitchen table to find the rust-red family-room couch. I sit, place the cup on the round side table, and then rest the computer on my lap. I push the little black power button, which is always hard to find in the dark. But eventually my finger slides over a dimple and when the screen glows, I'm ready for step two: music.

Without the right music, The Ritual serves no purpose: it's just waking up early. So I listen to acoustic vocals, which is key—literally. Instruments without electrical amplification and clear singing elicit muted feeling, coaxing emotion out from behind locked doors. And after a few minutes of listening, my brain changes; I feel it, a tickling where before there was nothing, so I scratch, then the itching becomes something more, an intense introspection. Obsessively writing is how I explore my psyche. This is The Ritual.

But this morning something is different.

Perhaps it's because I'm currently on deployment to Central Africa, confronting another manifestation of the world's evil? But no, The Ritual is not dependent on location—I've gone through the routine in many places. Why the loss of equilibrium? What is it that's changed this morning?

Suddenly, I feel something come loose; a past floats to my surface and then I realize what's different. This memory is not what I'm expecting, it's not part of The Ritual. I'm not thinking about Iraq this morning.

⚊

The airplane engine's purr is comforting, loud but soothing. Then suddenly the reassuring hum changes to an ominous sputter. Outside of the small round window the circle blur of the propeller slowly comes into focus . . . the propeller spin decelerates to . . . nothing. I press my left cheek to the window and look below; I see a sea of green. For hundreds of miles I see nothing but triple-canopy. I fall back into my seat and turn my head toward the other side of the fuselage . . . and count . . . one, two, and three, then thirteen heartbeats later the other set of propellers just . . . stops. It's silent, and the whisper of flowing air is tranquil; I'm soaring on warm thermals.

A few seconds later, I make sense of the hushed quiet.

I turn my head and make eye contact with the Sergeant Major who sits next to me. "Are we crashing?" I ask.

He responds with a nod.

Instantly my mind empties of everything—I know we're dying, so I feel absolutely nothing. After minutes of floating, we make a sudden hard left bank, and my cheek returns to the side window. Treetops flash by, and the pilot swivels and yells "Prepare for crash landing!"

I shut my eyes.

⚊

I open my eyes and then look over the dark hotel room. The clock now shines 4:34 A.M.

The memory this morning is from yesterday morning.

On a return trip from a small outpost in South Sudan, the statistically impossible happened: the wheels of the plane hit the ground, I'm thrown forward, and then back again as our plane hops over oncoming cars. When we come to a screeching sudden stop, I look through the cockpit's window, and to the front of us is a truck too big to move off the road. Fucking amazing—our engines stopped working within exact gliding distance of the only road that is just long enough, just straight enough, and just wide enough, for us to land in hundreds of thousands of square miles of nearly roadless jungle.

But my surprise is not about my unlikely survival; I'm accustomed to almost dying. What's really stunning is that I'm not thinking about Iraq this morning. Instead, as I sit in the dark of a Central African hotel room listening to Coldplay sing about a tangled spider web, I'm remembering a different, but more painful, moment in time. I'm remembering September 2011. It was then that two betrayals forced on me a binary choice—give up or choose life. That was when I chose a different path. That was when I instead chose to understand.

When I returned home from Iraq, I blocked everything out. I unconsciously chose to forget all of my wrong choices, all of the guilty and innocent people I caused to suffer. But I now realize that avoidance only makes things worse. No matter what I did, at some point these memories were going to come to the surface. What I needed was forced exposure, to confront each emotionally charged memory, gradually. What I didn't want, but so desperately needed, was to get back on the horse slowly, and to do this with my family sound asleep above me. That was the moment when I unconsciously created The Ritual.

In September 2011, when I was told to just go away, I found a new job in another part of Germany. We moved, and every morning since then I've awoken early to confront my

Enemy—each and every painful memory. This is my ritual, and it has been for more than three years.

The Enemy and I sit in the same room together and just glare from a distance. But over time something changed. One day I found I could look him in the eye. Then over time I discovered I could move my chair closer, millimeters at a time. Soon I was close enough to feel each breath on my cheek. That's when the screaming began, but over time the hate became loathing, then revulsion turned to disgust. Suddenly we're conversing, never friends, just enemies who are talking, suffering a different perspective. And when I thought I understood, I'd change my viewpoint. I'd stand up, move myself to another angle and start the process all over again. Over time the hurt transformed into just a problem, and that's when the nuances became debatable.

Then I'd start everything all over again, but with a new memory.

Over and over again, for three fucking years I did this, and after those countless therapy sessions I had with myself, emotionally laden memories became just facts. I edited the memories I couldn't get rid of. By sheer force of will, I revised myself.

Now, I'm finally able explain myself to myself.

I created a new life-saving narrative, and understanding—not forgetting, or reducing arousal, or using drugs—is how I came to forgive.

The Ritual is how I've moved beyond self-loathing: the jigsaw is reforming.

But no matter how hard I try, experiences from war will never just go away; my past is an intrinsic part of me. So I'll remain stunted, a marionette who struggles to make human connections. It just is, and I've accepted this. But how do I forever evade the old fear stirring, the fingernails tearing? It's called coping, waking up each morning committed to becoming a better person. The never-ending search for redemption is how I survive my purgatory.

A MOTHER'S PERSPECTIVE

by Lynn Russell Edmonds

The Iraqi wedding blanket hangs over the top railing of our stairs. A black border surrounds a myriad of bright colors and geometric shapes all bound together with irregular stitches. Tiny fragments of mirror reflect the surroundings. On my way up and down the stairs, I admire the shapes of flowers and animals that hint at the lives of those who painstakingly constructed the blanket.

On his Christmas break from Iraq, Bill and his girlfriend Amy gave us this blanket as a present. It's our family tradition to open the gifts together, one at a time, so we can all savor each gift that's given. My husband and I sat on the loveseat as we opened their present. Opposite us on the large sofa were Bill and Amy, and scattered across the floor and in other chairs was the rest of our diverse family. We "oohed" and "awed" marveling at the blanket's beauty, and wondered aloud about the lives of the women who created our gift, and their families. We pondered aloud what the clothing fragments were cut from: a husband's work shirt, a child's blanket tattered after years of loving, a woman's house gown splattered with cooking oils. Weeks later, several friends and I pondered where to put the blanket: safe in a drawer; hanging from a rod in the front room; covering a bed? We decided to drape it over the railing at the top of the stairs in the hope that each friend entering the front door would look up and enjoy the blanket.

The blanket was Bill's present, but he offered little more about his time in Iraq. Then he said good-bye and went to take long trail runs with a friend in San Luis Obispo. We were comforted to think he was reconnecting. Then his break was over, and Bill returned to Iraq.

We exchanged e-mails during his time in Iraq, but most of these were about his surroundings, his wonder at the deep history and religion of the area. We knew that he was imbedded with Iraqis and that there was a prison, but little else. He showed us some pictures of the Iraqis he lived with.

Back here in southern California, our lives continued as before. My husband officiated at track-and-field meets, delivered Meals-on-Wheels, and attended leadership meetings at the Episcopal Church. I was consumed with establishing a teen center to serve the youth in our small rural community of Fillmore. We were newly retired and enjoyed travel, visiting other countries, reconnecting with international friends. We e-mailed Bill details of our experiences in Finland, Switzerland, Italy, France, and Germany. We participated in an Iraq War protest in San Francisco. We felt we were supporting soldiers and him in particular. Bill didn't agree with that perspective.

I didn't understand why; we never understood Bill's desire to be in the military.

We had joined the Peace Corps immediately after our marriage in 1964 in part to avoid the Vietnam draft. Nevertheless, we supported his choice, and attended with pride and wonder all his military graduation ceremonies: boot camp, Airborne school, and Ranger school. We were proud when he graduated Special Forces and we bragged about it to all of our friends. He had always excelled at whatever task he'd undertaken and set very high expectations for himself. Bill was proud of the role he played in the life of our nation, and he'd probably say that American citizenship was a privilege that demanded sacrifice. So we supported his many deployments.

We e-mailed, mailed, and sent care packages to the many war addresses, and I often sent inappropriate items that would make him laugh: the brownies, oranges, and avocadoes that took months to finally arrive, moldy, in Iraq.

In Special Forces there wasn't much Bill could share with us, so we didn't press; but despite the carefree exterior we presented, we worried about our deeply caring and quiet son. When Bill deployed to Iraq, we weren't aware that he had volunteered. We just knew he was excited about it; he said it gave him an opportunity to support the Iraqis as they formed a new country.

But I fluttered around the computer, frantic if more than two days went by without hearing from him. And when we did get e-mails, I could tell he tried to be uplifting and encouraging, but Iraq made me particularly worried. I carried a heavy weight inside my chest. I was jittery and irritable; the mother of a Special Forces soldier never really knows what's happening with or to her son. His e-mails were short, intelligent, sometimes sharing his frustration, trying to help us picture his daily life, using humor to only hint at the dangers. He never mentioned a sniper or interrogations.

We thought we were supporting him, doing what we thought parents were supposed to do. But I now realize we absolutely failed to understand the toll war was taking on him; when he spoke about the history, about Islam and learning Arabic, his interpreters, the Iraqi guards he made friends with, it was all he was able to tell us of his experiences. I now realize he was trying to understand and make sense of what he was going through, and then share that without frightening us. We didn't give Bill the opportunity to share the darkness he was experiencing. We did not see his inner conflict.

When he came home from Iraq he seemed fine, but then we weren't looking for any signs of change. He seemed to be doing well, so we just continued on with our lives, and let him get on with his life. And the months soon became years.

We were so delighted when Bill met Cheryl and when later they married. We were overjoyed when they gave us one, later two beautiful granddaughters. We celebrated his earning a master's degree from the Naval Postgraduate School. When Bill was reassigned to Germany, we were pleased that he and his family would be able to experience a new language, a new culture, and new adventures. Life seemed happily normal.

Then one day in September 2011, I was sitting over coffee at our local Starbucks with friends, and I got a call. Our quiet son spoke for over an hour; disconnected thoughts, moving from delight to sudden sadness. He spoke of needing to make a lot of money, of leaving his family well off, of discovering a hidden mathematical formula. He spoke with long pauses and then bulleted speech. Goodness, he even described how he cried at a briefing. Thankfully, I had already planned a trip to Germany. I flew out the next week.

When I arrived, all seemed well until I realized that Bill wasn't sleeping. Morning after morning I would come into the kitchen for breakfast and realize he had been writing all night. Cheryl described his erratic behavior. He would cry for no apparent reason or become agitated over inconsequential events, all the while trying to understand his own responses. Fortunately, he has always been able to write about his thoughts, so he wrote and rewrote. I never knew he went to see a mental health counselor, or that when he moved across Germany, he was forced out of his job.

Through the months of writing, with Cheryl and the girls watching, Bill put his experiences into words on paper. Eventually, Bill shared his writing with me, and over the months and years I saw that his words became clearer about experiences I never had a clue about. I was saddened and angered by the situation our nation had put him in. I was devastated at the lack of support that we, his family, provided him.

Only because he decided to open up do we now realize the degree of his suffering, the depths of betrayal—we had entrusted our son to the U.S. government. This was the son that we had nurtured and protected as a child, then cherished and respected as an adult. And we neither knew nor understood the stresses, the terrors, the hard choices that Bill and other military members must make in war. Bill returned from Iraq a different person, but I just didn't know; that's hard for a mother to deal with.

I can give no deep clues or suggestions for those hundreds of thousands of family members whose loved ones are traumatized from many years of wars. But I now know that no war leaves the veteran untouched. My father returned from WWII with what my mother called "battle fatigue," and it took him thirty years to fully come home to us. Yet even with that experience, I can give no suggestions or recommendations. I am one small person in a small town in California, and I have only care and concern. I send my love to all of those veterans and service men and women and their loved ones who suffer from their experiences.

But I do ask myself:

Do we send our children to war because it's easy? Do we fully appreciate the horribly life-altering and forever consequences of our decisions? And when we do make this choice, do we assume the responsibility to provide the very best care for the veteran and their family?

I watch the city parades for returning military, the clapping passengers at airports, and the countless press conferences with the token war veteran. We put up a good front, but are we willing to buy one less fighter plane so we can better support them when they come home? Are the hundreds of millions of smiling and cheering Americans willing to personally sacrifice? As the mother of one of them, I'd answer: it seems like too many sons and daughters fall through the cracks.

The Iraqi wedding blanket still hangs from the stair railing, but it now has a completely different meaning. The mirrors reflect partial and fractured images. The scraps of clothing are just ripped, then torn apart. The stitches seem disjointed and uneven. The blanket isn't about some unknown Iraqi marriage. Instead it tells the story of war trauma and our nation's failed response. But I still straighten the blanket when it becomes uneven, and I wipe it clean of the clinging cat and dog hair; I want it to return to what I once thought it was. Sometimes I take it down and share it with friends. They appreciate the contrasts of colored cloth. I, however, admire what it's come to mean to us: the constant search for the ethical choice which is our son, and our collective responsibility to the hundreds of thousands of other American daughters and sons who we demand sacrifice from.

READING GROUP GUIDE

Discussion topics provided by George Lober, a Professor at the Naval Postgraduate School. Prof. Lober has, over this last decade and counting of war, taught, coached, and mentored countless Special Operation Forces Officers on ethics and morality before and after they deployed to war.

1. In *God Is Not Here*, Lieutenant Colonel Edmonds finds himself in a seemingly unresolvable dilemma. The Iraqi justice system will only convict and incarcerate prisoners who confess, but some hardened terrorists are capable of resisting interrogation, and they refuse to confess—unless they are subjected to torture. In addition, although torture may solicit a confession of past, present, and future acts, it's possible he will still be released back into society anyway. How would you advise LTC Edmonds under these circumstances? How would you advise the Iraqi interrogations of prisoners at the Guest House?

2. At one point, LTC Edmonds considers the possibility that executing a hardened terrorist may, on occasion, be the most ethical course of action. If the terrorist refuses to confess and,

as a consequence, the justice system returns the terrorist to society, many more lives may be lost, including the lives of both innocent civilians and fellow servicemen. However, if the terrorist is executed, society may well be better off, and those same lives may be spared. How would you advise LTC Edmonds in this instance, assuming that the evidence against the terrorist is overwhelming, the actions for which the terrorist was apprehended were both deliberate and brutal, and the justice system of the host nation in question—for a variety of reasons—often releases such prisoners back into society?

3. Eventually, LTC Edmonds comes to a hard-line compromise: he will permit coercive mental abuse but not coercive physical abuse. In your opinion, is there a justifiable discernment between the two? If so, what is it? Given the circumstances, could you accept a similar compromise?

4. Near the end of his memoir, LTC Edmonds suggests he is caught between two insensitive and broken systems of justice. The American military, he discovers, has little interest in investigating Americans who are implicated in torture, and the Iraqis with whom he works have little interest in protecting the human rights of the suspected terrorists they capture. In such an existential environment, he struggles to maintain his moral center and questions whether that struggle is worth the effort. If LTC Edmonds asked that question of you—whether or not, in your opinion, his moral struggle was worth it—how would you answer? What are the difficulties and disincentives, as you see them, to maintaining an isolated ethical position in such an environment? What coping mechanisms would you draw upon if you found yourself in a similar situation?

5. Is it ever ethically permissible to do the wrong thing for the right reason? How far should intentions factor in assessing

the "rightness" or "wrongness" of an act? How far would they factor in your determination to punish, or not punish, someone for violating a policy that forbids an act such as torture? What if the violation of that policy resulted in intelligence that clearly saved lives? Would that positive result influence your determination to punish or not punish the violator? Why or why not?

6. How would you personally define torture? What features, in your opinion, differentiate it from aggressive but justifiable interrogation? Does the degree to which an individual may be aggressively interrogated depend upon the offense that he or she is charged with committing, or on the import of the information they may have? Is a suspected terrorist who you believe has killed and will kill again more deserving of aggressive interrogation than someone charged with a lesser, non-capital offense? If so, why? What about other individuals such as hardened criminals, gang members, kidnappers?

7. In *God Is Not Here*, oftentimes only a confession prevented a killer from killing again. Therefore, if you knew that harsh, coercive physical interrogation could get a killer to confess, but that sometimes under such interrogation an innocent person would also falsely confess, would you consider such interrogations permissible? Would you authorize such techniques? Why or why not? Under what circumstances?

ACKNOWLEDGMENTS

To my agent Don Fehr and associate publisher Jessica Case, and all of the amazing people at Trident Media and Pegasus Books: thank you for hearing the small voice in the crowd. Your wisdom and tireless efforts are the only reason that *God is Not Here* became real.

ABOUT THE AUTHOR

Bill Russell Edmonds

Bill Edmonds, a lieutenant colonel in the U.S. Army, has served in various positions throughout the Department of Defense, the Special Operations community, and with other U.S. government agencies. A native of southern California, he first enlisted in the 75th Ranger Regiment in 1989, was later commissioned a second lieutenant in the Infantry, and joined the Special Forces in September 2001. With over twenty years of enlisted and commissioned service, he has multiple combat and operational tours on three continents. Bill received a bachelor's degree in International Relations from California Polytechnical University in San Luis Obispo and a master's degree in Defense Analysis, with an emphasis on terrorist networks and terrorist financing, from the Naval Postgraduate School in Monterey, California. He currently lives in Washington, D.C. with his wife, Cheryl, and two daughters, Natalie and Ava. This is his first book.